The
LEARNER-DIRECTED
CLASSROOM

Developing Creative Thinking
Skills Through Art

The
LEARNER-DIRECTED CLASSROOM

Developing Creative Thinking Skills Through Art

EDITED BY

DIANE B. JAQUITH
NAN E. HATHAWAY

Foreword by Patrick Fahey

TEACHERS COLLEGE PRESS

TEACHERS COLLEGE | COLUMBIA UNIVERSITY

NEW YORK AND LONDON

Material in Chapter 7 is copyright ©2011 from *Art Teaching: Elementary Through Middle School* by George Szekely and Julie Alsip Bucknam. Reproduced by permission of Taylor and Francis Group, LLC, a division of Informa plc.

Published by Teachers College Press, 1234 Amsterdam Avenue, New York, NY 10027

Library of Congress Cataloging-in-Publication Data

Empowering student-directed learning : developing creative thinking skills through art / edited by Diane B. Jaquith, Nan E. Hathaway ; foreword by Patrick Fahey.
    p. cm.
Includes bibliographical references and index.
ISBN 978-0-8077-5362-0 (pbk.)
    1. Art—Study and teaching. 2. Creative thinking—Study and teaching.
3. Student-centered learning. 4. Interdisciplinary approach in education.
I. Jaquith, Diane B. II. Hathaway, Nan E.
N350.E47 2012
372.5'044—dc23   2012023453

978-0-8077-5362-0 (paperback)

Printed on acid-free paper
Manufactured in the United States of America

19 18 17 16   8 7 6 5 4 3

Contents

Foreword

The couch provided more than just a comfortable place to rest or take a short nap. Cushions were lifted, rearranged, and carefully balanced to enclose space, a special space: a place large enough for a small child to ease into and dream.

These unique and tentative environments were my first attempts at fort building. The fascination I held for building with these cushions and their subsequent dismantling never tired. It did, however, take other forms. As I grew and acquired an increasing number of brothers and sisters, the demand for more elaborate and larger structures became evident. These new enclosures were tents, often formed from a table with a large blanket or sheet on the top that would touch the floor on all sides. There was something special about playing privately, free to make decisions without adult guidance.

Eventually these spaces moved outdoors and incorporated "grown-up" materials and tools, as well as new friends. The summer I was in 5th grade was particularly important to my construction history. My best friend Allen and I decided to build a fort so we could sleep outside during the hot and muggy Wisconsin summer nights. We decided that, rather than drawing up a plan, our first concern would be the gathering of supplies, materials, and tools. Our first expedition took us to a local freight company located just down the street, where we found two wooden pallets that would be taken apart to use like 2X4s. Our next acquisitions were the tools needed to take the pallets apart and reshape them into the skeleton of the fort. The task was formidable but accomplished with pride. Several visits to local grocery stores provided cardboard for the walls, and construction was ready to begin.

Allen usually acted as conductor, orchestrating these events. We dug holes with a shovel to hold the strongest pieces of wood to serve as pillars. Once securely in place, we nailed pieces of wood from post to post and at various angles to strengthen the building and provide the necessary support for the cardboard walls. We worked for most of the day, only taking a short break for lunch. Once all the cardboard was nailed to the frame, and suppertime approached, we carefully gathered the tools our parents had entrusted to us and made plans to meet early the next day for the finishing touches.

The next morning, with fresh energy, we laid out our plan. We painted the cardboard, cut holes in the walls for windows, and laid carpet scraps on the floor. It was Allen's idea to put in electricity. We plugged an extension cord into a house outlet and laid it in a small trench dug directly from the house to our fort. Allen got permission to use his father's old utility light to illuminate our hideaway at dusk. All in all, we considered it a job well done. We got a lot of use out of this fort, and other forts that we built. Whole afternoons were spent inside these as we occupied ourselves with various activities. We listened to the radio, plotted against neighborhood girls, traded baseball cards, or just hid from the world. We thought of these structures as magical, magnificent, and powerful.

I share my experiences here for the ways they can inform 21st-century teaching. The narrative clearly illustrates children engaged in self-direction, invention, problem-posing, problem-solving, critical thinking, and persistence. This summertime adventure provides insight into the "3Ps": play, passion, pertinence. Authentic art experiences, whether engaged in by master or novice, involve play, passion, and pertinence or purpose.

Artists, like children, are masters of play. Play encompasses experimentation, risk-taking, and invention, among other attributes. While working on our fort, many attempts were made to get it "just right." Those attempts often resulted in collapsed piles of wood and cardboard, but eventually our creativity provided guidance to success. Artists seriously involved in their work are passionate. While working to complete our fort, we had a vision and worked tirelessly until it was realized. Nothing could distract us from our mission.

While artists create for many reasons, their attempts are usually focused and filled with intent. Because our investigation into construction was self-conceived and personal, it had purpose and pertinence. Our forts were refuges for dreaming, recounting tales, creating stories, telling secrets, and defending our newly defined space. Intent provided structure for our making. Sometimes we planned and sometimes our play and experimentation, our doing, or praxis, grounded our ideas. The opportunity to conceive our ideas in multiple ways was important to our success and inspiration, as it is with all artists.

The Learner-Directed Classroom provides the opportunity for art educators to consider how the qualities of play, passion, and pertinence can be acknowledged and embraced in the atmosphere of bureaucracy and testing prevalent in our schools today. In the following chapters, practitioner-researchers provide narratives of experience that demonstrate an investigative, process-oriented exploration of concepts, materials, approaches, and techniques. Self-direction and invention permeate these stories of student learning. The authors remind us that talk about 21st-century skills and creativity has to be more than lip service. The time is now to empower students and make them responsible for their learning. Arguments that a choice-based approach to learning is not compatible with the demands of schools today are dispelled by the authors. Assessing students, aligning curriculum, recognizing and accommodating all learners, talking about student work, and choice-based art for elementary and middle schools are examined. These discussions are grounded in real-world practice. This is especially helpful for educators considering transitioning to a student-directed curriculum.

Similar to the autonomous actions of my fort-building adventures, students engaged in constructing their educational experiences develop self-sufficiency, are more open to risk-taking, become more adept at reflection, and are confident in refining their evolving ideas. Motivation becomes increasingly intrinsic, allowing the teacher to act as a guide or facilitator—an essential element in a student-directed curriculum. Understanding art history and art from other cultures is not ignored; rather, it is delicately woven into the interests and needs of the students as the opportunity arises to introduce and discuss this information. Assessment is not abandoned. It is an ongoing, genuine, reflective process grounded in observation and understanding. Self-direction leads to the development of the inner critic. While evaluating our forts, Allen and I recognized that this process of assessment was necessary to our quest for bigger and better forts. Finally, the authors demonstrate that in an environment where students chart their own plan for learning, the problem of how to teach the exceptional learner seems to disappear because learners of all abilities are supported to create from individual interests and strengths.

If we are honest in our quest to grow 21st-century skills in our students, we must provide them the opportunity to play, experiment, fail, consider, reconsider, collaborate, invent, share ideas, and, most importantly, the *occasion* to determine their own quest for knowledge and understanding. *The Learner-Directed Classroom* provides educators with possibilities for making this happen.

Patrick Fahey
Colorado State University

Acknowledgments

From the Editors: This book is a collection of real-world teaching and learning experiences in classrooms from across the country. We are indebted to the authors for their willingness to share their stories and their patience throughout the long process of making a book: Catherine Adelman, Marvin Bartel, Katherine Douglas, Patrick Fahey, Ellyn Gaspardi, Clyde Gaw, Lois Hetland, Pauline Joseph, Tannis Longmore, Linda Papanicolaou, Cameron Sesto, George Szekely, Ilona Szekely, and Dale Zalmstra.

We are greatly appreciative of the staff at Teachers College Press: Brian Ellerbeck, whose vision for our work led to clarity and purpose, and Lori Tate, whose guidance has been invaluable during the production process.

We wish to thank our readers, whose insights and comments helped to shape the direction of this anthology: Christine Phillips, Cindy Bencal, Georgia Smith, and Yael Zakon-Bourke.

We are grateful for the goodwill of our families, who have graciously acclimated to our excessive time conferencing about this project. To Diane's family, Maurice, Lia, and Luke; and Nan's family, Izzy, Libby, and Hannah, we thank you. Nan also extends gratitude to her very first art teacher, Margaret C. Hathaway—thanks, Mom.

We thank our students past and present, who are and always have been our very best teachers. We are appreciative of our school communities for their support and trust. We are thankful for the hearty administrative support we have received from Barbara Mitchell Hutton, Tom Drake, and Richard King.

Lastly, we wish to acknowledge Katherine Douglas, whose extraordinary leadership and commitment to choice-based art education has resulted in the dynamic international professional community, Teaching for Artistic Behavior. Our work is the result of numerous collaborative interactions with like-minded colleagues in this organization to develop and improve student-directed art education. These exchanges were made possible due to Katherine's steadfast vision of shared practice to meet the needs of both students and teachers, who, without such a group, would be working in isolation. We also thank the many members of TAB who inspire us every day with their wisdom and insightful approach to choice-based art education.

Introduction

Diane B. Jaquith
Nan E. Hathaway

Art class is where I can picture ideas and what will come out best for me instead of someone else picturing it for me. Being able to choose my work allows me to take time to think about what I want to design. My brain gives me options for different ideas to follow based on what I know I am good at. I can get my work to a place where it feels just right to me. (10-year-old boy)

The collection of writings in this anthology offers inspiration and guidance for educators who would like to provide self-directed learning opportunities for students to inquire, think divergently, and engage in work that has personal relevance. Children have an abundance of ideas—most of which never make it into school, where there is little opportunity for outside ideas to develop. When children can consistently direct their work in school, their ideas flow and develop over time. With practice, children are adept managers of their creativity and capable of far more than adults require of them. Schools can and should be welcoming places for students' original ideas.

Schooling has evolved into a prescriptive, data-driven bureaucracy where the system rewards convergent thinking. Literacy and numeracy skills may be improving nationwide as a result of standardization, but not without a cost. Today's high school and university educators see far less divergent thinking and creative problem-solving than in the past. "Don't get sick," one medical school professor advises, "because if your illness is not in the book, the new doctors can't help you." Likewise, industry leaders cite concerns over the decline in creative thinkers who will keep our economy healthy and competitive (Bronson & Merryman, 2010; Pink, 2006). To address this deficiency, educators should find a balance between direct teaching and independent learning so students have sufficient opportunity to inquire, engage, discover, apply, and evaluate their own ideas.

The need for education to focus on contemporary skills, including creativity, innovation, invention, communication, and collaboration, is adequately and elegantly defended by leaders in the field (Partnership for 21st Century Skills, 2004; Robinson, 2010; Zhao, 2009; see also McNulty, 2010; Warlick, 2010; Wolk, 2011; Zimmerman, 2009). This direction, known as the 21st Century Skills movement, has gained tremendous attention from motivational speakers Daniel Pink and Sir Ken Robinson. Their message calls for teachers and administrators to address contemporary skills and attitudes that are needed both now and for the future.

As districts implement initiatives for creativity and innovation, administrators and teachers wonder what this will look like in the classroom. This anthology offers vignettes of PreK–8 visual art classrooms where students regularly engage in self-directed inquiry through problem-finding and solving, reflection, and evaluation. In these learning environments, innovative practices promote creativity through strategies that engage learners. The authors included here are practicing and retired teachers, researchers, and members of the higher education community who value authenticity in education. Their writing presents a compelling case for learner autonomy.

The content is organized into four parts that support transition into self-directed learning environments: Planning for Paradigm Shift, Supporting Learner Autonomy, Special Considerations for Special Populations, and Thoughts on Reflection and Assessment. The spotlight is on art educators, whose domain is open to creative teaching and learning, though there are lessons here for all educators who strive to support independent learning habits in the classroom.

PLANNING FOR PARADIGM SHIFT

To promote student autonomy, all aspects of teaching and learning are examined through the lens of transformation. In this part, teachers describe the transition into learning environments that encourage student experimentation and discovery. Class structures, including instructional practice, norms, routines, and schedules, transform to accommodate diverse needs and interests. The learning environment goes through reorganization for student accessibility and contains materials, equipment, and visual resources. Substantive change is a reality to meet the demands of creative and critical thinkers.

Self-directed learning shifts the locus of control from teacher to student and for those accustomed to prescriptive lessons, this might feel threatening. Administrators can acknowledge this and support their staff as they transition into a different way of teaching. School leaders who understand that contemporary skill acquisition is process-oriented, not product-driven, will recognize that students are highly engaged in discovery learning. The work itself will be unique and reflect the interests and ability of the student, not the teacher.

SUPPORTING LEARNER AUTONOMY

Students need a genuine voice in the content, process, outcome, and assessment of their learning so they can take ownership of their education. The authors in this part focus on children's innate ability to discover, explore, and expand individual interests.

In dynamic creative learning environments shaped by student input, intrinsic motivation activates self-challenge and engages learners (Deci & Ryan, 1985), resulting in unique applications of knowledge. Teachers' roles become that of facilitators, not "transmitters of huge bodies of knowledge" (Weitz & Suggs, 2000, p. 133). Knowledge gained through first-hand inquiry is powerful. Learners with autonomy develop personal paths for skill and knowledge acquisition, eventually becoming metacognitive about their process. In settings designed for self-direction, students set the course for learning.

SPECIAL CONSIDERATIONS FOR SPECIAL POPULATIONS

The measure of a learning program can be made by the way in which it accommodates exceptionality: students who lie outside the norm, do not conform, are right or left of center, require accommodations, or exhibit unique characteristics that affect teaching and learning. For these populations, a flexible, self-adjusting learning environment is paramount. This part highlights several distinct populations of students who work to their strengths while building skills and confidence. By design and in practice, learner-directed environments provide access for students of all abilities while celebrating differences and accommodating the disparate needs—be they physical, emotional, intellectual, sensory, or spiritual—of diverse populations.

THOUGHTS ON REFLECTION AND ASSESSMENT

Introspective teachers are keen observers and note nuances to inform instruction. They use formative assessments to understand how their students learn and where to place emphasis. Authors in this section speak about the decisions teachers make in their instruction and questioning practices, resulting in analysis and reflection on the relationship between teaching and learning. Just as students develop skills and understandings through self-directed inquiry, their teachers evolve in their insights about the learning process. The art classroom examples in this part provide practical models that demonstrate how creativity, innovation, invention, communication, and collaboration skills—important to all disciplines—progress through self-directed learning.

CONCLUDING THOUGHTS

The Learner-Directed Classroom illustrates and interprets many of the concepts previously presented in the book *Engaging Learners Through Artmaking* (Douglas & Jaquith, 2009) by offering concrete examples of classrooms and programs that implement student-directed pedagogy. Many of the authors in this anthology teach for student autonomy through the philosophy of the Teaching for Artistic Behavior (TAB) organization. This pedagogy, often referred to as choice-based art education, is a studio-based approach that recognizes students as artists. Choice-based education shifts creative control of learning and its products from teacher to learner to amplify student voice and heighten engagement. The choice-based learning environment develops community to facilitate for essential understandings, concepts, and skills. This pedagogy is not new. Two of the authors, Pauline Joseph and Katherine Douglas, independently pioneered learner-directed practices and laid the foundation for this pedagogy decades before the TAB professional learning community existed.

Student-directed learning experiences permeate the art programs described in this anthology, and offer a promising direction for authentic learning across disciplines. Forward-thinking administrators and teachers know that the future of education depends upon innovation in teaching and learning. Just as we ask our students to take initiative, we ask that teachers do the same: to question, experiment, create, and reflect as educators and leaders who fully engage with the learning process.

REFERENCES

Bronson, P., & Merryman, A. (2010, July 19). The creativity crisis. *Newsweek*, *CLVI*(3), 44–50.

Deci, E. L., & Ryan, R. M. (1985). *Intrinsic motivation and self-determination in human behavior*. New York: Plenum Press.

Douglas, K. M., & Jaquith, D. B. (2009). *Engaging learners through artmaking: Choice-based art education in the classroom*. New York: Teachers College Press.

McNulty, R. J. (2010, October 11). Keynote address to Washington West Supervisory Union. Harwood Union High School, Mooretown, VT.

Partnership for 21st Century Skills. (2004). *A framework for 21st century learning*. Available at http://www.p21.org

Pink, D. H. (2006). *A whole new mind: Why right-brainers will rule the future*. New York: Riverhead Trade.

Robinson, K. (2010). *Bring on the learning revolution!* Retrieved from http://www.ted.com/talks/sir_ken_robinson_bring_on_the_revolution.html

Warlick, D. (2010, November 22). Education reform is reestablishing, redefining, and retooling. *2 Cents Worth: Teaching and learning in the new information landscape*. Retrieved from http://davidwarlick.com/2cents/?p=2817

Weitz, G. M., & Suggs, M. S. (2000). A field guide for art educators: Guerrilla tactics for change. In D. E. Fehr, K. Fehr, & K. Keifer-Boyd (Eds.), *Real-world readings in art education: Things your professor never told you* (pp. 127–136). New York: Falmer Press.

Wolk, R. A. (2011). *Wasting minds: Why our education system is failing and what we can do about it*. Alexandria, VA: Association for Supervision and Curriculum Development.

Zhao, Y. (2009). *Catching up or leading the way: American education in the age of globalization*. Alexandria, VA: Association for Supervision and Curriculum Development.

Zimmerman, E. (2009). Reconceptualizing the role of creativity in art education theory and practice. *Studies in Art Education, 50*(4), 382–399.

Part I

PLANNING FOR PARADIGM SHIFT

Schools are complex communities, layered with policies, procedures, and traditions that season the expectations of every stakeholder. In most subject areas, there is little latitude in curricular choices; even the delivery is often scripted. As critical and creative thinking skills appear more frequently in district goals, art educators will need to transform their practice to transfer ownership of learning to their students.

Chapters in this part discuss the transition into a learner-directed practice with experienced recommendations for implementation. Each of these authors began his or her career in a teacher-directed practice, but realized early on that this approach did not value the unique capabilities of each child. Concurrently, top-down pedagogy seemed at odds with authentic artistic exploration and innovation fueled by the creator's own passions and curiosities.

Katherine Douglas draws upon her 35 years of experience to provide a proactive rationale in "Advocating for a Student-Centered Art Program: Navigating Expectations." For educators who wish to increase learner autonomy, Douglas guides readers past potential pitfalls and challenging constraints through careful planning, timely communication, and support systems. Administrators, colleagues, and students, as well as parents and the community, are recognized as partners in the transition to a learner-directed pedagogy.

Among the factors that place real restrictions on teaching and learning is the school schedule. Choice-based art programs are more accommodating of scheduling issues because the room setup remains consistent, despite the age level of the students. In Chapter 2, "Time as a Choice in Self-Directed Learning," Diane Jaquith walks readers through the structure of a typical class, and offers a formula for optimal learning time. Discussions about choices made by students most frequently focus on media and subject matter; Jaquith examines the equally important, yet less obvious, student choice of how to utilize time for individual creative purposes.

The need to differentiate curriculum drew Linda Papanicolaou to implement a learner-directed environment that she details in her personal reflection, "Engaging Middle School Students Through Choice-Based Art." Like most choice-based teachers, Papanicolaou revised her routines to accommodate developmentally appropriate expectations and site-specific requirements. The act of transferring ownership to the learner is transformative for both teacher and student.

In the final chapter of this part, Pauline Joseph describes how, by reorganizing the learning environment into a "Visual Resource Studio," students readily access materials, tools, and references for their work. Art visuals, embedded into centers, provide opportunities for students to develop relationships with past and present artists. Joseph explains how both direct and indirect teaching with rich visual exemplars enables learners to connect with the global art community.

This part provides a foundation for preservice teachers and those wishing to transform their practice. For those who have already transitioned into learner-directed pedagogy, each chapter offers suggestions and salient considerations to improve teaching and learning at all levels.

CHAPTER 1

Advocating for a Student-Centered Art Program

Navigating Expectations

Katherine M. Douglas

Art teachers electing to transform their practice face many internal obstacles—changes in routine, letting go of early teacher training, and moving beyond knowing and controlling everything that will happen in the studio classroom. Initiating these moves and changes requires time, study, and some initial successes with students. When the teacher offers students the opportunity to be in charge of their own learning, and when the students realize that this is actually the case, there will be many encouraging behavior changes. Children who resist teacher direction or who have trouble sitting still for extended periods of time thrive when set on their own path. The interactive nature of choice-based pedagogy, with differentiation embedded into all aspects of the practice, allows teachers and students to find what works best for them and to learn from each other.

Outside influences, expectations, and preconceptions necessitate an advocacy campaign in support of student-directed learning for the new choice-based teacher. Some preparation and a proactive stance in these areas can go a long way to support a studio-learning practice. All stakeholders, including students, administrators, colleagues, parents, and members of the community, need clear information about the goals and outcomes of the art program. The teacher new to choice-based teaching should anticipate potential questions from the school community, and prepare to communicate with clear goals and accounts of positive outcomes.

STUDENT EXPECTATIONS

Students expect to be told what to do at all times in school. Even 5-year-olds quickly learn they must stay in line, raise their hands before speaking, and wait patiently for directions before beginning anything. Over time, most students accept the necessity of compliance, putting their own interests and ideas aside and looking to the teacher for inspiration. In contrast, children in choice-based programs are practicing skills of self-regulation and independence as responsible and self-propelled artists. Choice-based studios contain organized centers for available media, as well as comprehensive resources for access by students as needed. Classes begin with brief whole-group demonstrations of techniques, media, concepts, and art history. Students may work with the new focus or independently in one of the centers, where materials and techniques have been introduced in previous whole-group demonstrations.

The art teacher needs to be explicit—both about the structure of the classroom and about the freedoms open to the students. "In this studio your ideas can be the basis of your artwork. Here is where you will find and learn to use materials that you need to communicate what you want to say visually." The longer students have been in school, the more difficult it may be for them to look to themselves for artmaking ideas because of the impact of school norms on creative thinking. Students whose art experiences have been carefully planned by the teacher have experience in following directions, but little practice in having an idea and choosing a way of expressing it (Gaspardi & Douglas, 2010). Individual creativity is like a muscle, and if unused for any length of time, atrophy must be overcome. Teacher encouragement and a safe environment for experimentation, play, and making mistakes supports the reinvigoration of the artistic excitement common in children before they enter school (Gaw & Douglas, 2010).

ADMINISTRATOR EXPECTATIONS

In some districts the visual art supervisor observes and evaluates the art teacher—in others, the principal or assistant principal is the supervisor. In the case of a principal as evaluator, the choice-based teacher will need to proceed carefully *and* proactively. As the instructional leader, it is the principal's job to assume responsibility for the quality of teaching in each classroom; however, many administrators lack knowledge about art education pedagogy. The allure of dazzling class sets of teacher-designed artwork on hallway bulletin boards can distract from the important issue of authentic learning. It is essential for the choice-based teacher to help the administrator see beyond the finished product to the far more important processes, decisions, and authentic learning that take place in student-directed work.

Choice-based art teachers work within school requirements to create an organized method for communicating with busy administrators. Lesson plans for learner-directed pedagogy contain the same information as traditional ones, but are created for use all year long (Douglas & Jaquith, 2009). These plans are similar to a unit plan, for which the objectives focus on students being able to create artwork independently, from start to finish. Working backward from this goal, the teacher lists skills and procedures to be introduced over time in demonstrations, such as color-mixing on a palette, setting up a painting space, choosing subject matter, or correcting mistakes. Vocabulary, lists of resources, and related discussion topics can be part of this document. Lesson plans corresponding to the current demonstrations can be kept on a clipboard for easy access when an administrator visits. Simple curriculum maps are a great help to both teacher and administrator. On a one-page grid, major media and topics are noted in boxes under each grade level. This can be posted in the classroom or in the teacher plan book for easy reference.

Planning

Traditional teacher plan books, arranged with squares for each class period, remain an effective note-taking device. Art teachers, particularly at the elementary level, may have hundreds of students, and this can help to keep track of individual needs. With each class noted, it is easy to keep the plan book open to the next week's page. Notes about specific material needs or concerns about a student are jotted there to be available for the next time that group is in the studio classroom. These notes are also helpful reminders for guidance meetings and offer impressive evidence of the complexity of differentiating for as many as 900 students per week.

Substitute plans are an important communication tool, and the administrator might be interested in a copy. A well-drawn map of the choice studio, along with an outline of class procedures, can reassure your principal that teaching for artistic behavior comes with structure and lots of organization. The substitute folder can also contain a valuable resource—a group photo from each of the many classes, with student names attached. Easily available on a clipboard, these photos really help to attach names to faces.

Visual Resources

A teacher feeling administrative pressure should make sure that some of the signage in the centers also speaks to adults. Good domain-specific vocabulary and studio center directions are silent teachers (Hathaway, 2008), not only for students, but also for visitors to the studio classroom. Visual art standards can be displayed in a large format where appropriate. The Partnership for 21st Century Skills (Partnership for 21st Century Skills, 2009) is a detailed resource listing supports for outcomes needed in the society of the future. Studio habits (Hetland, Winner, Veenema, & Sheridan, 2007) are another strong resource for student-directed pedagogy that deserves a place on the classroom wall. When students are encouraged to *envision* or *engage and persist* (two studio habits), and this is made explicit via room signage, it can help adult visitors to see student work through that lens. The good news about preparing this information for administrators is that it will become a valuable tool for the teacher to self-evaluate and to grow as a choice-based teacher.

ART DEPARTMENT EXPECTATIONS

In larger school districts, art teachers are members of a department, often with music colleagues. If there are differences in teaching and learning approaches within the department, the contrast between student-directed goals versus teacher-directed goals can make for discomfort all around. The choice-based teacher who frames studio-based learning in a positive way without implying criticism of other teachers will have more success within the department. If colleagues do not feel threatened, they may be curious enough to ask questions and visit. Although choice-based teachers can successfully adapt the district curriculum for learner-directed pedagogy, the approach and outcomes may be quite different from those in traditional didactic programs (Gaw & Douglas, 2010).

SCHOOL COLLEAGUE EXPECTATIONS

In many schools classroom teachers expect the art teacher to not only connect with classroom curriculum, but to become its illustrator. Social studies, science, and math instruction certainly benefit from the addition of hands-on use of art supplies, but an art teacher who creates the art curriculum as a picture of academic classroom work will miss opportunities to fully address visual art standards. At the same time, students will miss opportunities to work as artists. As with administrators, the choice-based teacher can highlight for classroom colleagues the benefits of student learning over the production of pre-designed products.

Classroom Teachers

With more and more classroom time designated for test preparation and data collection, it is understandable that teachers might ask the art teacher to shoulder projects that they used to do themselves. Good communication supports authentic integration. The choice-based art teacher who is familiar with social studies themes at each grade level can provide resources and references at the appropriate time. Art room demonstrations that link to classroom curricula can be arranged to meet the goals of the art program first while facilitating for interdisciplinary connections. It is important to keep the art program focused not only on visual art standards but also on the needs of students to practice with media and techniques to create individual, meaningful work. As with administrators, a proactive stance with classroom teachers can go a long way to promote collegiality and support for the art program.

Special Needs Staff

One often successful collaboration with non-art teachers comes through the special needs staff. Depending on the school program, it is valuable to invite speech and language therapists, occupational therapists, and learning disability teachers into the studio classroom. These specialists often find that their students excel in a setting where they can choose their work and start from their strengths. Some special needs teachers may be able to work alongside their students in the comfortable atmosphere of the studio while providing mandated support. These specialists often note that they get to know their students better by observing and working with them in art.

The choice-based art teacher is frequently cited as someone with unique insight into the positive abilities of at-risk children (Douglas & Hathaway, 2007). Even the most challenged students exhibit preferences for particular materials. Children with academic or physical needs are often closely supervised by adults throughout the school day. In the studio classroom these students make choices about their work spaces, materials, and the content of their work. The structure of learner-directed environments is aligned with the Universal Design for Learning (National Center on Universal Design for Learning, 2009), which calls for multiple modes of transmitting information, multiple options for students to show what they know, and making connections to student interests and ideas. In the choice-based art setting, many students with special needs have success not seen in their other classes.

PARENT EXPECTATIONS

Teacher-directed art projects appeal to many parents because they believe the products represent their child's ability and creativity. The carefully managed step-by-step traditional school art experiences leave little in student control; instead, the results conform to an adult aesthetic. Parents are often pleased with these polished results and some art teachers take pride hearing of parents visiting the frame shop with art that they, the teachers, imagined and designed. Authentic child art often contains unique or idiosyncratic subject matter and shows skill development in its early stages. It is easy to understand that parents may be puzzled or upset when youngsters in a newly begun choice-based program arrive home with art that truly reflects their age, interests, and beginner's art ability.

Communication

With the opening of a new choice studio, the teacher can implement a carefully planned school-to-home outreach. An attractive newsletter provides an overview of the purposes of choice-based teaching. It is important to highlight the learning involved when students self-direct their work: planning in advance, deciding on appropriate media, working through mistakes and challenges to a conclusion, reflecting on the success of the work, and considering future paths. School websites offer another venue to display and explain the choice-based program. Frequent updates highlight centers as they open, newly introduced tools and techniques, connections to visual art standards, and art happenings outside the school. Photos of students and their work-in-progress, glimpses of centers, and closeups of finished pieces provide visuals for this simple school-to-home connection. Information on developmental stages of artmaking is very useful to parents; hints for talking about children's artwork will help parents better understand early efforts and make children feel the importance of their work.

Open House and Conferences

Open House school events and parent/teacher conferences provide excellent opportunities for parent education. If the teacher is in the habit of snapping digital photos during art class and encouraging students to do the same, there should be plenty of material to create slide shows for visiting parents. Whether or not the art teacher assigns a grade, the report card is another communication venue. A brief printed insert for each grade level can describe centers available and major units of study, and cite connections to visual arts standards and district goals. Although art teachers rarely meet with each parent, it is important to create some form of record-keeping for those conferences they do have. Charts marked by students each week provide an easy-to-maintain record of the centers each child has visited. Teachers whose students keep portfolios of work will find these useful for parent meetings. It is likely that choice-based teachers will hear from parents who state that while they don't understand just what is going on in the studio, their child looks forward to art class more than ever before!

COMMUNITY EXPECTATIONS

Art teachers navigate requests from the community, which holds its own expectations for both teachers and students. It is common, for example, for local groups to connect with art classes with poster-making requests. Teacher mediation of these demands will deflect conflicts with studio learning goals. A choice-based teacher has the option to announce outside projects, give a demo on rough drafts, and discuss the qualities of the product, in this case, a good poster. A center can be set up to accommodate students who are interested in participation. Tell both students and adults that one role of artists in society has been to give their talents to the good of their community. Teachers can be flexible in adapting various community requests for posters, scenery, and decorations to offer more options for interested students, while creating valuable support for the art program (Andrews, 2005). A good relationship with members of the local community has many benefits—taxpayers gain an appreciation for the hard work of the teachers and the abilities of the students. An art teacher with vigorous outreach can truly make the school and the art program look good.

EXHIBITION EXPECTATIONS

Exhibition is a valuable component of choice-based practice. Students who choose work for display are experiencing authentic self-assessment. The creation of accompanying artist statements allows the student to reflect on process and to share ideas with potential viewers. In Massachusetts, the state visual art standards require students to select work for display as part of the reflection and assessment process (Massachusetts Department of Elementary and Secondary Education, 1999). In student-directed classrooms, teachers turn over much of the planning, selection, and display of artwork to students, whose choices might be different from what their teacher would select. This can be disconcerting at first, but the rewards and deepened student learning are worth the change. Exhibition is an integral part of art learning; choosing art for display is embedded in the work of the artist.

The choice-based art exhibit can be one of the most exciting parts of the school year. Good planning before the exhibit will allow students to decide which pieces will represent them to the community-at-large. Because student-directed work may differ substantially from what adults are used to thinking of as art, an interpretive exhibit is essential. Artist statements, written by the children or scribed by adults and older students, accompany all exhibited work in choice-based art programs. When adult volunteers assist in the creation of an art show, they have the opportunity to experience the thought processes of the children through their artist statements. As a result, these parents will become strong advocates for the show and for the art program in general. When high school students (often from the art club) work with younger students, it is a valuable experience for all, and can open avenues of communication with secondary art teachers. Photos of children at work and written materials explaining the choice-based approach make the exhibit both an event and an episode of learning for all viewers. Choice-based teachers find that the enthusiasm of the students for an exhibit that truly reflects their work and interests is one of the greatest public relations successes for the art program.

CONCLUSION

The creation of an arts-based program requires energy, patience, and courage. It is both exciting and scary to be part of a new paradigm of teaching. This responsive pedagogy is created and re-created through trial and error, as the teacher learns from the students. Given broad responsibilities, students respond to high expectations. The artistic behaviors of these students and resulting idiosyncratic work reward the teacher who garners support for the program. As a means for both student and teacher learning, choice-based pedagogy never ceases to challenge and elevate learning.

REFERENCES

Andrews, B. (2005). Art, reflection and creativity in the classroom: The student-driven art course. *Art Education, 58*(4), 35–41.

Douglas, K. M., & Hathaway, N. (2007, March). *Think about it: How school rebels and others find success in the choice-based art class.* Session presented at the 47th annual convention of the National Art Education Association, New York.

Douglas, K. M., & Jaquith, D. B. (2009). *Engaging learners through artmaking: Choice-based art education in the classroom.* New York: Teachers College Press.

Gaspardi, E., & Douglas, K. (2010, June). *Art education for the 21st century*. International VSA Arts Conference, Washington, DC.

Gaw, C., & Douglas, K. M. (2010, March). *States of play in the choice-based art room*. Paper presented at the meeting of Child's Play, Children's Pleasures: Interdisciplinary Explorations, Hofstra University, Hempstead, NY.

Hathaway, N. (2008). 10 teaching and learning strategies in a "choice-based" art program. *Arts & Activities, 144*(1), 36–37.

Hetland, L., Winner, E., Veenema, S., & Sheridan, K. M. (2007). *Studio thinking: The real benefits of visual arts education*. New York: Teachers College Press.

Massachusetts Department of Elementary and Secondary Education. (1999, November). *Massachusetts arts curriculum framework*. Available at http://www.doe.mass.edu/frameworks/arts/1099.pdf

National Center on Universal Design for Learning. (2009). *UDL guidelines, version 1.0*. Available at http://www.udlcenter.org/aboutudl/udlguidelines/introduction#intro_learners

Partnership for 21st Century Skills. (2009). Available at http://www.21stcenturyskills.org/index.php

CHAPTER 2

Time as a Choice in Self-Directed Learning

Diane B. Jaquith

Time in educational environments is a precious currency for teachers and their students. The schoolhouse clock, generally under the purview of adults, carries tremendous implications for teaching and learning. Mandates, pacing guides, and standardized testing determine the distribution of time throughout the year, both in curriculum and the school schedule. Hours and minutes have become so tightly guarded that barely a few moments trickle down for prized *unstructured time* when students can arrange activities for their own purposes. Self-directed time is often used by classroom teachers as a carrot to coerce compliance, such as additional minutes for recess, and students gravitate toward any such occasion where they can control their time and activities.

Tight restrictions may meet administrative requirements but are antithetical to authentic learning. Flexible time in educational settings enables students to independently construct meaning and understanding through inquiry and problem-solving (Beghetto & Plucker, 2006). Schools that value creative thinking provide opportunities for students to learn how to self-direct their ideas while working within the classroom context. In these arrangements, students self-regulate time to pursue their own ideas and make meaning of the world they live in. When the school day is tightly scheduled into literacy blocks, math blocks, and tiered intervention blocks, it becomes a challenge to also designate time for creative work on a regular basis. Constructivist theory reconsiders how time is allocated for deep learning by encouraging flexible, not rigid, timelines (Brooks & Brooks, 1993) that support creativity in schools.

This chapter will highlight choices that self-directed learners make with regard to the pace of their working habits and the duration of their activities. When students are consciously aware of their time usage, they can learn to manage it more efficiently for their own purposes. To understand effective teaching structures that facilitate for independent time management, it is helpful to examine a model for self-directed learning in art education.

CLASS STRUCTURES THAT PROMOTE AUTONOMOUS LEARNING

In the choice-based learning environment, art teachers plan the class period to maximize time for independent artmaking. Studio centers and routines remain consistent for every class, enabling students to plan ahead, or to engage in discovery learning through materials exploration (Douglas & Jaquith, 2009). Regularity is essential for students to orchestrate their learning. A predictable routine enables even young children to anticipate their self-directed activities. Since schedules vary tremendously between schools, the following guidelines provide optimal studio time in choice-based settings:

- 10–15% of class time for whole-class instruction
- 70–80% of class time for self-directed studio work
- 10–15% of remaining class time for cleanup, sharing, and self-assessment

Teachers who see students daily may front-load instruction at the beginning of the week and increase minutes for sharing and self-assessment later in the week, thus extending self-directed time midweek. The goal is to preserve significant time for independent learning. The following analysis details the organization of typical choice-based class structures through the lens of real time.

Whole-Class Instruction

In choice-based teaching and learning, instruction is delivered first to the whole class, followed by small-group and individual instruction during studio work. Concepts, techniques, and visual culture are among the topics covered briefly with the entire class. Instruction activates student learning while reinforcing expectations for high standards. The lesson may be a catalyst for artmaking, opening doors for further exploration that day or later. As the year unfolds, relevant topics emerge out of students' work and are incorporated into the curriculum. Thoughtful planning guides teachers to meet instructional objectives to deepen understandings in students' independent learning and encourage new inquiry.

Self-Directed Studio Work

Students are eager to get into studio centers where their work is ongoing and the materials are inviting, and to create alongside classmates. Decisions about how to utilize studio time are usually good ones—learners practice skills, often repeating past efforts with growing competency. Some research a topic of interest while others plan and gather materials. Many retrieve work-in-progress, reflect on next steps, and continue. Collaboration with peers is organic, as children have flexibility to group and regroup according to needs. Because this work is personally relevant, children who typically require multiple supports in the classroom can often work independently. Occasionally a student may abandon or defer artwork in favor of a promising new direction. If productivity appears to decline, teachers intervene and help to redirect. Students who are intrinsically motivated by activities of their choosing and have full autonomy over content and media are highly engaged (Jaquith, 2011), and find that their studio time passes by all too quickly.

Cleanup, Sharing, and Self-Assessment

With the responsibility of self-directed learning comes the commitment to care for one's work and the studios. Artists place their artwork in designated safe locations. They have been coached to distinguish among the leftover materials, returning those with potential for reuse, and discarding that which cannot be repurposed. Efficiency is enhanced when boxes for materials, tools, and reference materials are clearly labeled so students know exactly where to return these resources. While waiting for everyone to complete their cleanup tasks, children convene in predetermined areas to share their work or to document their progress in writing. With practice, the transition time between cleanup and departure is managed effectively. Closure becomes an ideal moment to highlight efforts that reflect the day's learning objectives.

READINESS AND EXECUTIVE FUNCTION

Ideally, all students will easily transition between activities, plan their work, organize materials, and self-regulate their behaviors throughout each class. In reality, students' readiness determines their ability to move independently through each class structure. While the majority of children are able to manage self-directed learning independently, those with deficits in executive function may need assistance to develop self-regulation skills.

Cooper-Kahn and Dietzel (2008) describe executive function as "an umbrella term for the neurologically-based skills involving mental control and self-regulation" (p. 10). Children with learning differences develop strategies to support executive functioning deficits in initiation, working memory, planning, organization, and self-monitoring (Cooper-Kahn & Dietzel, 2008). Students who think divergently and generate good ideas might lack skills that enable them to carry those ideas through planning, goal-setting, and preparation, as explained by Dawson and Guare (2004):

> Time management is a higher-level executive skill that includes a number of components such as the ability to follow and make a schedule, to plan and organize, to estimate how long it takes to complete tasks, and to monitor progress in the course of completing tasks to ensure that one is "on schedule." This is a very difficult skill for many to learn because youngsters with poor time management skills tend to lack not only the ability to estimate how long it takes to do something but also lack a sense of *time urgency*—or the concept that something needs to be completed in a timely and efficient manner. (p. 60)

Some students could feel overwhelmed with the responsibility of self-directing their work because their ability to independently set goals and self-monitor is compromised by "lagging skills" (Greene, 2008, p. 11). Or the student may need support transitioning between activities, what Greene refers to as "a shifting cognitive set, required any time a person moves from one task to another" (p. 16). These "lagging skills" might appear in self-directed work to be a lack of initiative or ineffective use of time. Strategies such as step-by-step planning, peer assistance, and visual reminders enable these learners to successfully manage their independent work. In choice-based learning environments, students practice executive functioning skills independently, to gain confidence and experience. Through frequent repetition, procedures and strategies become integrated practices for self-regulation (Cooper-Kahn & Dietzel, 2008; Deci & Ryan, 1985), enabling students to gain autonomy over their time with or without supports in place.

LEARNER-DIRECTED PACE

Activities overlap continuously throughout the learner-directed classroom, creating a textured momentum that engages young artists in compelling endeavors. Students differentiate their learning by choosing their activity and setting their own pace, the rate at which they conduct their work. For example, markmaking with drawing tools can elicit a slow and methodical rhythm for one child and a burst of unrestrained energy for another. Finding one's optimal level of challenge keeps students focused and on task (Deci & Ryan, 1985; Jensen, 2008). Those who can complete a task easily challenge themselves with greater complexity. They may be working alongside a classmate who takes longer to reach similar goals. Individuals with a strong inner clock can synchronize their activities to coincide with the classroom clock. Others check in with their teacher or a classmate to find out how much time remains. Because everyone's work is unique, there is no competition or race to the finish line.

Work habits vary among self-directed learners, and their teachers come to associate particular artistic behaviors with individual students. Some artists need significant time to get started on their work, envisioning and planning on paper first. Clay artists often play with their materials to see what they can form before settling on an idea. Across the room, an artists' cohort confers in great detail over the narratives emerging in the drawing studio. The teacher monitors each learner's progress, and students may check in frequently with their teacher as well, seeking reassurance and affirmation for their efforts.

DURATION OF ACTIVITY

The duration of any self-directed art activity will vary according to the purpose of the endeavor. A few students will be engaged in a long-term activity that, on and off, could span the entire school year. Others, particularly younger children, will rush through their work in a frenzy, completing three or more artworks each day. A few might play with materials and choose to save nothing. Most, however, exhibit a variety of endurance behaviors, which include both brief and sustained output appropriate to their purposes, as described by Eisner (2002):

> Work in art is typically directed by an idea that is realized in the materials and through the form that the artist creates. These ideas can be large or small, important or trivial; they can reveal what has gone unseen, or they can put the familiar into a context in which it can be re-seen in a new and vital way. (p. 51)

In self-directed art classes, artistic process (versus product) is the focus of teaching and learning. Students' efforts, especially with play and practice work, can easily be misconstrued as unsubstantial by teachers new to this type of pedagogy. When questioned, young artists may have difficulty defending their authentic artmaking habits. The patient teacher will heed the words of Bayles and Orland (1993): "The function of the overwhelming majority of your artwork is simply to teach you how to make the small fraction of your artwork that soars" (p. 5). This rings true for the choice-based art classroom, where short-term and long-term activities are ongoing for all students.

Short-Term Activities

Many young children are content with simple attempts that meet their needs through the successful realization of their idea. It is only when adults suggest that they spend more time on their work that children may feel that their efforts are being judged. Young artists respond through spontaneity when a memory is triggered or if an art material calls for improvisational play. An airplane constructed of two craft sticks or a gestural painting defies the need for additional time. In fact, the original concept may be destroyed through a well-intended intervention. Instead, the teacher can discover repetition in a collection of work and behaviors of a child who works quickly. These patterns are evidence of solid learning through play and practice work, despite the seemingly fleeting attention to individual artworks.

Play. Children experience the world through play and through the social actions inherent in play (Gaw & Douglas, 2010; Szekely, 1988), rehearse and develop ideas. For example, young children who are exploring tempera paint in the absence of a specific assignment can often be observed mixing every conceivable color and then happily blending the colors together on their paper. This playful behavior results in developing understandings about color theory. When encouraged, these children may become the most enthusiastic painters, unaware that viewers may not recognize the complexity of thought in their initial work.

In the classroom, play can be loud and attract adult concerns about intentions. Szekely (1991) comments: "To children, play is serious business. Through play, they express what they know, clarify concepts, and organize their knowledge" (p. 2). Play, a catalyst for divergent thinking, generates ideas for creative problem definition (Runco, 2007). It is through play that creative ideas emerge and evolve into long-term activities. Two 4th-grade girls with strong interest in drawing planned stop-motion animation about a family outing to the beach. They carefully drew their characters and, through play, developed an engaging narrative about children swimming with dolphins. In order to bring their story alive, the girls had to experiment with photography and digital animation media. In the process, these students developed skills in collaboration, storytelling, and technology. Children who work together playfully enjoy challenging themselves and each other, and in the process, can lose track of time altogether.

Practice. Like an open sketchbook, practice work shows evidence of developing skills, Lowenfeldian *scribble stages* in each media (Douglas, 2004; Hathaway, 2006) that describe emerging efforts. Students new to self-directed learning go through transitional phases, often sticking with familiar safe choices of content and media. For example, young adolescent girls may be observed drawing their names over and over again. After all, one's name is indisputable and, as some students relate, there is great satisfaction in varying the design of the letters through color, shape, and pattern. Resources on calligraphy and typography, with a brief introduction, will broaden these students' understanding of graphic design and visual communication.

Practice also comes in the form of imitation, with students mimicking a particular technique or content that is seen in classmates' work and displayed exemplars. In children's work, it is not uncommon to see portions of drawings crossed out, the object in question redrawn next to the original attempt. Practice leads to confidence, which then leads to risk-taking, necessary small steps for independent work since "timidity is not conducive to creativity" (Nickerson, 2008, p. 413). Young artists know that most of their work is not intended for exhibition—for them, it serves as visual expression—for their teachers, it is pure evidence of learning.

Increasing Duration. Teachers watch for appropriate moments to move short-term artmaking into longer, sustained efforts. Tina, a 3rd-grader who loves to work with recycled found objects, always brings in raw materials and leaves the same day with a completed object in hand. One day she arrived with her favorite 10'' doll. "I need to make her a house!" she exclaimed. Offered a large box on the condition that, due to the size of the project, she would dedicate at least three classes to the dollhouse, Tina eagerly agreed. She worked with the attentive care of an interior designer, selecting her materials carefully and revising her ideas as she took scale into consideration. In this case, the teacher's mediation capitalized on Tina's intrinsic motivation. Through encouragement, she experienced a long-term activity in which she had adequate time to pursue and reflect upon her work with a sense of pride in the satisfying outcome.

Long-Term Activities

Self-directed learning gives students the option to spend significant time on one artwork or to create a series that addresses a particular theme. Strong intrinsic motivation can sustain an activity over prolonged time. Extrinsic motivators can also perpetuate long-term work, such as when peers collaborate (Jaquith, 2011). The enjoyment gained from social interactions while working collectively can extend a project into many months. In one class, two 2nd-grade boys resumed structural designs practiced in 1st grade to build a large-scale tower. They related their process to their classmates:

> We started with two small craft stick pieces that we took home and then brought back to school. We did these a lot in 1st grade so we decided to put them together to make a big structure. Daniel did a complicated thing with crossing over sticks that is near the bottom. There are balconies and random shapes. The last thing we added are these aluminum foil shooting stars and comets.

In this case, the teacher eventually intervened when the originally defined problem was more than adequately solved; it was at this point that the boys added the celestial elements to complete their work. Here, the purpose of intervention is to encourage new directions for learning because over the course of a school year, studio time is a precious and limited resource.

Perseverance or Abandonment

When learners reach a critical point in their work, they have two choices: Give up or persevere. The studio habit of *engage and persist* (Hetland, Winner, Veenema, & Sheridan, 2007) drives an intrinsically motivated child, even in the face of failure, to continue by quietly pursuing the issue or by enlisting help. Others might choose to abandon the work altogether. Artwork may be consciously discarded, temporarily abandoned, or simply forgotten. Those who abandon their artwork might do so through frustration that accompanies failure or to follow a better direction. Understanding the reasons for abandonment provides insights into the artist's unmet needs or artistic thinking, such as:

- Impatience—lack of immediate results
- Insufficient resources—the right materials are not available
- Skill readiness
- Failed collaboration
  * More people are needed but not available
  * Creative differences
- Perception of insufficient time for completion
- Waning interest
- Dissatisfaction with results
- Original concept leads to new insights

Teachers who feel threatened by these actions may fear that abandonment reflects poor instructional practices or waste of materials. This is rarely the case; as stated previously, artistic purpose dictates the direction of independent learning. One-on-one conversations unearth intentions behind abandoned work. For instance, children like to recreate real-world objects, like cars, but may voice frustration if the wheels fail to work properly. When limited technical skills impede student success, teacher intervention can help to salvage the work. On occasion, work is abandoned because students just need a break from a long-term activity, deferring to a different short-term endeavor. Most often, however, the pursuit has already served its purpose and the artist has moved on.

REFLECTION

Artists constantly reflect on their work-in-progress to adjust and refine their original ideas. The careful observer can catch students in the act of reflection—there is a silent pause as the hands stop—then they resume activity with renewed focus. The studio habit *reflect* (Hetland et al., 2007) helps students to translate their visual thinking into verbal response. Children can learn to ask themselves the following questions, which can be posted for all to see.

For work-in-progress:

- What do I like about this artwork?
- Do any existing parts need more of my attention?
- What is my goal for today? How will I meet that goal?
- What resources will I need to complete this artwork?
- How will I know when this artwork is complete?

For completed work:

- If my artwork had a title, what would it be?
- Why did I choose to make this?
- Has my original idea changed? If so, in what ways?
- What other things have I made that are similar to this?
- What do I hope people will notice when they look at my artwork?
- What will I do next?

Reflective thinking requires frequent practice to become integral in students' creative work. As a result, learners may discover patterns in their artistic process through this kind of self-inquiry, leading to deeper self-awareness as artists.

TIME FOR CREATIVITY

Self-directed play, practice, sustained activity, and reflection provide an open-ended framework for critical and creative thinking. Establishing real time for these activities in the school day means that education must slow down and take stock of what is really important. Holt (2002) builds a case for "slow schools" by describing the loss of experiential learning, comparing data-driven schooling to the culture of "fast food." The Slow Movement embraces play as an authentic learning opportunity, but time for play is brief in so many American schools that narrow the curriculum. Honoré (2004) makes a plea for a more holistic approach to learning:

> Rescuing the next generation from the cult of speed means reinventing our whole philosophy of childhood, much as the Romantics did two centuries ago. More freedom and fluidity in education, more emphasis on learning as a pleasure, more room for unstructured play, less obsession with making every second count, less pressure to mimic adult mores. (p. 271)

Due to the compressed nature of school schedules, creativity rarely gets the time it deserves. Placing time limits on creative work may inhibit the very behaviors that teachers hope to enhance (Antes & Mumford, 2009; Runco, 2007). Researchers, including Csikszentmihalyi (1996) and Amabile (1996), have developed paradigms for creative work in which divergent thinking leads to problem definition, inquiry, evaluation, and eventually, a finished solution. Divergent thinking in service to problem definition necessitates more time than that of a typical classroom brainstorming session because creative ideas incubate over time. Incubation, or simply "time away from a problem" (Perkins, 1981, p. 50), provides the necessary distance to consider the problem out of context. In art classes, time for incubation actually benefits by the school schedule, because students typically leave their work until the next scheduled class. Those who are deeply invested will continue to envision their plans while away from their work.

When students self-direct their learning, they have autonomy to act upon reemerging concepts that spiral back into conscious decision-making. Powerful learning can result when students regenerate interest or apply understandings to new situations (Rostan, 2006). In the self-directed learning environment, students can revisit ideas or engage with concepts and techniques that were previously out of reach. It is not uncommon for a student to follow a line of inquiry over several years, both at school and at home, with increasing sophistication in skill and concept. In this way, learners apply new knowledge to existing understandings as they construct meaning and make connections.

CONCLUSION

Preservation of an effective student-directed learning environment requires vigilance on the part of the teacher, who quite often is working against the currents of the fast-paced school culture. In schools where every piece of the curriculum, including the arts, is prescribed, time for students to assert and develop their voices is compromised. By empowering students to choose the content, media, pace, and duration of their work, teachers provide autonomy and time to practice self-regulation. Self-directed learners in control of their time develop technical, cognitive, and social skills; build knowledge; and construct meaningful connections through authentic learning experiences.

REFERENCES

Amabile, T. M. (1996). *Creativity in context*. Boulder, CO: Westview Press.

Antes, A. L., & Mumford, M. D. (2009, April-September). Effects of time frame on creative thought: Process versus problem-solving effects. *Creativity Research Journal, 21*(2/3), 166–182.

Bayles, D., & Orland, T. (1993). *Art & fear: Observations on the perils (and rewards) of artmaking*. Santa Cruz, CA: The Image Continuum.

Beghetto, R. A., & Plucker, J. (2006). The relationship among schooling, learning, and creativity. In J. C. Kaufman & J. Baer (Eds.), *Creativity and reason in cognitive development* (pp. 316–332). New York: Cambridge University Press.

Brooks, J., & Brooks, M. (1993). *In search of understanding: The case for constructivist classrooms*. Alexandria, VA: Association for Supervision and Curriculum Development.

Cooper-Kahn, J., & Dietzel, L. (2008). *Late, lost, and unprepared: A parents' guide to helping children with executive functioning*. Bethesda, MD: Woodbine House.

Csikszentmihalyi, M. (1996). *Creativity: Flow and the psychology of discovery and invention*. New York: Harper Perennial.

Dawson, P., & Guare, R. (2004). *Executive skills in children and adolescents: A practical guide to assessment and intervention*. New York: The Guilford Press.

Deci, E. L., & Ryan, R. M. (1985). *Intrinsic motivation and self-determination in human behavior*. New York: Plenum Press.

Douglas, K. M. (2004, April). *Exhibits that honor choice: Teaching for artistic behavior*. Session presented at the 44th annual convention of the National Art Education Association, Denver, CO.

Douglas, K. M., & Jaquith, D. B. (2009). *Engaging learners through artmaking: Choice-based art education in the classroom*. New York: Teachers College Press.

Eisner, E. W. (2002). *The arts and the creation of mind*. New Haven, CT: Yale University Press.

Gaw, C., & Douglas, K. M. (2010, March). *States of play in the choice-based art room*. Paper presented at the symposium Child's Play, Children's Pleasures, Hofstra University, Hempstead, NY.

Greene, R. W. (2008). *Lost at school: Why our kids with behavioral challenges are falling through the cracks and how we can help them.* New York: Scribner.

Hathaway, N. (2006). Is there a scribble stage for sculpture? *School Arts, 106*(4), 38–39.

Hetland, L., Winner, E., Veenema, S., & Sheridan, K. M. (2007). *Studio thinking: The real benefits of visual arts education.* New York: Teachers College Press.

Holt, M. (2002, December). It's time to start the slow school movement. *Phi Delta Kappan, 84*(4), 264–271.

Honoré, C. (2004). *In praise of slowness: Challenging the cult of speed.* New York: HarperOne.

Jaquith, D. B. (2011). When is creativity? *Art Education, 64*(1), 14–19.

Jensen, E. (2008). *Brain-based learning: The new paradigm of teaching.* Thousand Oaks, CA: Corwin Press.

Nickerson, R. S. (2008). Enhancing creativity. In R. J. Sternberg (Ed.), *Handbook of creativity* (pp. 392–430). New York: Cambridge University Press.

Perkins, D. (1981). *The mind's best work.* Cambridge, MA: Harvard University Press.

Rostan, S. M. (2006). A young artist's story. Advancing knowledge and the development of artistic talent and creativity in children. In J. C. Kaufman & J. Baer (Eds.), *Creativity and reason in cognitive development* (pp. 244–268). New York: Cambridge University Press.

Runco, M. A. (2007). *Creativity theories and themes: Research, development, and practice.* Burlington, MA: Elsevier Academic Press.

Szekely, G. (1988). *Encouraging creativity in art lessons.* New York: Teachers College Press.

Szekely, G. (1991). *From play to art.* Portsmouth, NH: Heinemann Press.

CHAPTER 3

Engaging Middle School Students Through Choice-Based Art

A Personal Reflection

Linda Papanicolaou

When my children were young, they attended a school where their art teacher hung the hallways with class sets of children's artwork, along with a museum reproduction of the painting that was being studied: Dufy flowers, Picasso cubist collages, and similar artworks. Although they were colorful and appealing, something about them nagged at me. Eventually, I was able to put my finger on the problem: All those "in the style of" lessons are a didactic formula that teaches students *about* art through the lens of other artists' aesthetic visions rather than giving them an authentic artmaking experience. As art teachers know, the products of this kind of assignment appeal to adult eyes and aesthetic tastes, but all too often neglect meaningful connections to students' own artistic interests and inclinations.

I have been a middle school art teacher for 10 years and am now in my 5th year with a choice-based program. What follows is a description of my personal experiences with this method: what led me to it, how I implement it in my classroom, how it addresses considerations such as state standards, and how to balance between product and process.

CURRICULUM AND SCHEDULING CONSIDERATIONS

Six years ago, my curriculum looked like that of our district's other two middle schools. For incoming 6th-graders there was the "Wheel" class that rotated every 5-1/2 weeks, covering Art, Computers, Drama, Home Economics, Industrial Technology, and Languages. The Wheel served as a sampler introducing students to the elective classes available to them in 7th and 8th grades. Art 1A, a foundational class with discipline-based lessons in a variety of media, was offered to 7th- and 8th-graders. With Art 1A as a pre-requisite, Art 1B was an advanced class intended to prepare serious students for the art program in high school.

From the beginning, this curriculum was a poor fit for my school community. Our student body is about half the size of the district's other two middle schools, and our master schedule is organized around academic core teaming. Parents expect an elective program similar to the other schools. Yet, due to our size, we cannot offer every elective in every period, and the students on a given team will not have access to all the course offerings. Add the district's contractual obligation to tenure loads, as well as the increasing need to put struggling students in academic support classes, and the result is an all-consuming nightmare at registration time.

The effect on my classes was that the integrity of sequential 1A/1B art courses could no longer be maintained. Each semester, several returning students were placed in the beginning class, and beginning students were assigned to the advanced class. Sometimes beginners' skill levels were higher than those of returning students, and often the advanced class was hampered by the inclusion of students who had little interest in art but were there because this was the only available elective that fit their schedule.

For Art 1A, I tried changing assignments from semester to semester so that students who cared enough about art to repeat the class would not be bored. This became burdensome; it was not always possible to design and deliver four different lessons for each concept. Art 1B posed a more difficult problem. Unable to assume a common experience or skill level among the students in Art 1B, I could not teach it as an advanced class. Moreover, students who had not taken art after their initial exposure to middle school art on the Wheel were flourishing in the high school art program. Clearly, the 1B class was not a requisite for success in high school art, yet to abandon the curriculum sequence would send the wrong message about my art program.

What to do?

"You're going to have to differentiate," said a district-level administrator.

How?

I signed up for staff development seminars on the *Elements of Instruction* (Palo Alto Unified School District, n.d.) to learn about differentiation. The instructors were surprised to see an art teacher in attendance, believing, I suspect, that the elements of instruction were not germane to my practice. I learned a lot of useful things about formulating and teaching to objectives, anticipatory sets, active engagement, and monitoring, but I came away feeling that reading and math style groupings would be detrimental to the studio community. In my attempt to nurture my students, I was still missing a crucial concept—that there was a way to teach art other than through teacher-directed, whole-class assignments.

The breakthrough for me came when, through one of my online art education discussion groups, I learned about the Teaching for Artistic Behavior organization and found colleagues who were grappling with familiar problems in their own practice. In my years with teacher-directed, whole-class art, I had already learned how important it was to leave scope for student decision-making in my lessons, so moving student choice from the periphery to the core of my teaching method was almost inevitable as the next step. Within a semester I had developed a class routine that provides both structure and flexibility.

CLASS STRUCTURE

Our daily schedule is staggered so that classes meet 4 times weekly for 55 minutes. I divide my class period into three segments as described below.

Opening Demos and Exercises (15 minutes on average)

As students enter, they encounter a prompt on the screen and we begin with a brief instructional exercise. Early in the semester, I open centers and use this time to practice setup, cleanup, and independent work with focus and intent. As the semester progresses, this time evolves into foundational drawing, skill-building, aesthetic discussions, art history, and reflection/critique—in other words, the strands of modern, discipline-based art education.

Choice Time (35 minutes on average)

As students finish the opening activity, they move to various centers. Drawing, painting (tempera and watercolor), calligraphy, ink-brush painting, origami, collage, fibers, and computer studio centers are always open. Clay, in an outdoor work area, is available unless it's raining (in California we don't have much of a winter). Papier-mâché, altered books, stained glass, weaving, or acrylic painting may open and close as the semester progresses and student interest waxes and wanes. Commonly used tools and supplies are placed strategically around the classroom where students can get whatever they need. Special items, such as X-acto knives, small brushes, glitter, and feathers, are kept in the closet and monitored by me. During Choice Time I circulate among the worktables, monitoring, troubleshooting, offering feedback, and modeling critique while also watching the clock and planning cleanup.

There is always Choice Time. If the opening activity is going to be long on one day, I alert students in advance so they can plan, and I shorten opening work the next day. The result is committed students who have assumed agency over their art time. With the many different activities typical of a choice-based studio, the room may look chaotic to the uninitiated, but the level of student engagement is high and productive routines are in place.

Cleanup and Closure (5 minutes)

We're often so engaged that it's hard to stop artmaking. I try to calculate how much time each group will need and call cleanup on a staggered schedule. Five- or ten-minute advance warnings help students to budget their time and make the transition. Sometimes students spontaneously burst into a cleanup song they remember from elementary school!

Before dismissal I check the classroom and provide a short closure: summarizing, or asking some students to show everyone their work or to share special ideas they've developed. For continuity, it helps if we plan and clarify the instructions for the next day. In this classroom environment, students are active participants who help shape their own learning.

IMPLEMENTATION OF CHOICE-BASED ART EDUCATION

In the transition to choice-based art, there will be a period of adjustment as teachers and students, parents and administrators, all become familiar with the new roles and expectations of this kind of classroom. Following are a few things I've learned about implementing a choice-based art program at the middle school level.

Tools and Materials

Because I don't have to invest in class sets of everything, supplies go farther, better materials become affordable, and I can provide equipment that is expensive or bulky to store, since not everyone is doing the same thing at the same time. We have two computers, a bamboo tablet and a scanner, three pottery wheels, an extruder, a slab roller for the clay station, and easels for acrylic painting. This equipment increases the authenticity of the studio experience and heightens student interest.

Assigned Seats and the Arrangement of Stations

The room is furnished with eight tables that easily accommodate four students each. My seating chart is alphabetical so I can take roll quickly. Students sit at their assigned tables during opening activities and roll, but during Choice Time I encourage them to regroup with others who have chosen the same activity. Middle schoolers are so inherently social that they voluntarily seek to work with friends and help each other. Unless too many people wind up at the same table, or the talking adversely affects artmaking, I let them sit where they wish.

Opening and Closing Stations

Every class has its unique interests and personality. In one period there may be six students at a new center, and in the next period none. In a week, that may change, or it may not. I've learned to be flexible and let the students show me what they need and want.

EXPANDING THE CURRICULUM WITH VOLUNTEERS AND VISITING ARTISTS

In a choice-based classroom, learning takes many forms. We have had a preservice art teacher organize an acrylic painting station, a parent teach ink-brush painting, and traditional Chinese crafts. Guest speakers give presentations on topics such as fused glass, film, and computer graphics.

Empowering Students as Instructors

I've learned to rely on the students who are experienced with working at a center to orient newcomers. For this to work well, my opening demos must be structured to emphasize information that is not only to be used now, but to be passed on as well—for instance, tearing the paper small for papier-mâché, or the use of scoring and slip for joining clay.

Also, I've learned that not everyone has to do a particular project for learning to take place. Sometimes I suggest that students walk around and see what everyone else is doing. Inspiration can come from peers as well as the teacher. Engaged students are good observers, and a quick glance over someone else's shoulder may be enough to plant an idea for the future.

Dealing with the Risk-Adverse

There are always two or three students who are hesitant to stray from their comfort zone. These students may only want to draw the same thing over and over. I don't confront them but quietly look for ways to nudge them to broaden their ideas or expand their skills. Those who love army battles with stick figures may like to learn how to incorporate three-dimensional landscape and more complex figure types; others who decorate their sketchbooks with hearts or names in bubble letters may like to try crayon batik, glue line and chalk drawing, or value blending with colored pencil for variety. Reluctance to go beyond a certain comfort level is a matter of learning trust, which is itself an artistic behavior. Creative risk-taking is an area of growth that can be worked on over the semester.

MEETING STATE STANDARDS THROUGH CHOICE-BASED ART

One of my early concerns was whether and how this teaching approach would meet state standards. But choice-based art education is standards-based. State standards do not require that every child demonstrate understanding by doing the same lesson or making the same project. Standards are about perception, discussion, analysis, and creation. They address the very things that are the strength of a choice-based classroom.

I wince at the memory of one of my old whole-class painting assignments. It was a favorite done by other teachers in our districts, and the projects turned out so well that I decided to display our class set in the office. When students' written labels read, "Then we were told to . . ." I was horrified. Had I over-directed everyone without really engaging them? My students' description of the project helped me to realize that in teacher-directed art, there will always be students who happily follow directions and produce show-quality work, but following directions is what has been taught. The opportunity for students to make authentic artistic decisions has been at the edges at best. Indeed, my students were being honest when they wrote that they were doing what they had been told to do.

My guiding principle now is that what I have taught has not truly been learned until it appears in the art that students themselves initiate. All my lesson objectives are approached in this context. We no longer do formulaic discipline-based art education (DBAE) assignments in which students learn about famous artists by imitating them. Rather, when a master artist's work becomes relevant, I bring out examples and say "Here, other artists have addressed the same problem; this is how they handled it."

EXHIBITIONS AND ASSESSMENT

When I first began choice-based teaching, one of my biggest concerns was the districtwide exhibition in our local art center each May. I vividly remember the first student-choice painting I selected to hang: an Impressionist-style landscape of a girl in a white dress amid wildflowers. This painting was unique—not the product of a teacher-scripted lesson, and it had *heart*. My fear was that a work of authentic children's art would not be well received when all my colleagues were showing clustered examples of well-honed, teacher-directed DBAE-style art lessons. Since then I've developed an exhibition style that includes works of student choice, assigned exercises, and photos of students engaged in artmaking. In addition, I include signage that explains the Teaching for Artistic Behavior philosophy and describes the artistic behaviors I routinely see in my classroom: exploration, problem-solving, working for improvement, and pursuing ideas through extended series.

Gradually, the way I assess students has also evolved. In the beginning I used a rubric with a scale of 1 to 5 for various things such as work habits, portfolio and presentation, understanding concepts, use of materials and class time, and contribution in the studio community. I never particularly liked this as an assessment tool, believing that it was both too blunt and too complicated to encompass the diverse styles, abilities, and developmental levels typical in middle school. Then it occurred to me that these are all aspects of artistic behavior. Wouldn't it strengthen the learning experience if the students assessed and evaluated themselves?

To provide opportunity for self-assessment, periodically I assign reflective writings on topics such as "What is one thing you as an artist would like your viewer to know about this art work?" or "Describe a problem you faced in making this art work and the solution you found." I also conduct oral assessments and ask students to "Show me how you used one of the principles of design in one of your art works." Finally, as the grading period ends, I require students to complete a simple checklist rubric with specific questions about ways the student has exhibited artistic behavior in class. I've been gratified that the students all seem to answer honestly and even tend to be a little too exacting on themselves.

CONCLUSION

Originally I came to choice-based art because of scheduling and curriculum concerns, as well as a need to provide differentiation in my classes. What I found was a teaching methodology that allows me to enter realms in the experience of art teaching I could not have imagined. In the beginning, I was astonished at how desperate the students were for the respect and validation that choice gives to their own thoughts and aspirations. Often they seemed fearful that choice would be taken away again. I had to reassure them frequently that no, Choice Time is every day in our art room.

The longer I work with middle school students, the more I understand that they are at a unique stage of life, one that has its own unique concerns, and I no longer worry so much about preparing my students for the high school art program. I tell them about it, listing all the things they'll learn if they continue, but in my classroom the focus is on what they want and need in the here and now.

The biggest change I have observed since converting to choice-based art education came when our school revised the 6th-grade Wheel schedule, changing the rotation to include just four subjects for a full quarter each. This became an incentive for me to discard the old sampler class and remake the art portion of the Wheel to be more like the 7th/8th-grade elective class. With more sustained time with the students, and the liberation from whole-class projects, I was able to move my foundational 3-D and figure drawing demos down to 6th grade. Here the instruction feels more age-appropriate and becomes enthusiastically incorporated into the students' free-choice work. The 7th- and 8th-graders now arrive in the art elective on day one knowing what they want to do with their Choice Time, and I have revised my curriculum maps for those classes to include more advanced material. Ironically, the Wheel has become my foundational class and I have now attained that course sequence so elusive in the old way of doing things.

At the same time, I am reaching deeper into my own knowledge of art. In the process, I learn as much or more from my students as they from me. My classroom is a place of joy and of daily creative epiphanies. No one ever says, "I'm finished, what do I do now?"

REFERENCE

Palo Alto Unified School District. (n.d.). *Elements of instruction.* Workshop Booklet, Palo Alto Unified School District, Palo Alto CA. Available at www.gunn.pausd. org/staff/EOI_Booklet.pdf

CHAPTER 4

The Visual Resource Studio

Embedded Art History
and Appreciation

Pauline Joseph

Art history and appreciation are the sticky wickets of art education, competing with studio work in the curriculum for precious time and resources. Art educators' art history knowledge originates in a deep-rooted interest in artistic process and history. The ability to place both process and history into context while teaching grows with practice. This is an invaluable goal for learner-directed pedagogy, resulting in readily accessible visual resources in the classroom through prepared exemplars and the immediacy of the Internet.

In learner-directed environments, attentive teachers design the space to embed facets of art history within each media center and the classroom as a whole. The classroom transforms into a visual resource studio with the teacher actively facilitating for relevant art history connections with emergent student work. In traditional visual art curricula, lesson plans tie selective art history to teacher-directed products. Rather than expecting art history to be reflected in children's artworks, self-directed students connect with the artwork of the human species through their own work. This important distinction allows children to understand the visual relationships between their work and the work of established artists and expands their ability to sense and navigate these relationships.

THE MEDIA CENTERS APPROACH

The media centers approach did not come out of a vacuum—the concept was influenced by educators who came before. Art education in the 1960s expanded to include art history and criticism in the curriculum (Efland,

1990). At the time I was invited by Dr. Al Hurwitz, my department chair, to assist in the creation of curriculum to cultivate art appreciation. We designed a variety of visual art games that specifically spoke to art history and developed strategies to activate students' curiosity. Gaitskell and Hurwitz (1970) describe this "discovery" methodology:

> Instead of providing the pupils with answers prior to the discussion, the teacher sought to elicit responses by posing questions that centered about a single conceptual problem—the ways in which artists differ in their work. In order to deal with such a problem, the children had to become engaged in such processes as visual discrimination, ordering, comparison, classification, and generalization. (p. 433)

The curriculum included field trips to galleries and studios in metropolitan Boston to further enrich students' knowledge of contemporary art.

During the era of open classrooms in the 1960s and 1970s, British infant schools strongly influenced American education (Barth, 1974; Gross, 1971), giving rise to the era of Open Education. This philosophy entered classrooms where teachers acknowledged that they were having all the joy in creating lessons with little residual excitement left for students. It didn't seem fair for teachers to hold onto the creative part of learning. Innovative teachers understood that students were missing the core of artistic process and that it would be necessary to empower them with control. In order to do so, these teachers would need to align with like-minded school administrators who could provide support and resources to further their goals of learner-directed pedagogy, as described by Barth (1974):

> The principal's position of responsibility and leadership within the school is the critical and pivotal point of influence over teachers' teaching and children's learning. It is not sufficient for the administrator to permit teachers to innovate. If teachers are to move toward open classrooms, the principal must actively, deliberately, and carefully facilitate their efforts. (p. 176)

I was one of those teachers, and Dr. Roland Barth was one of those administrators. He advocated for Open Education in the same school district where I was teaching both studio art and art appreciation. So, in 1975, I sought him out to be my principal.

"THINGS WILL BE DIFFERENT NEXT WEEK"

Once settled into Barth's elementary school, I alerted students that things would be different when they returned to art class the following week. After consulting with and incorporating pedagogical support from Dr. Barth, a dedicated student teacher and I spent the weekend designing media centers with art materials, tools, and visual resources.

The space was arranged into seven learning centers including drawing, printmaking, fiber arts, painting, clay, construction, design, and eventually an eighth center for computer drawing. Filled with neatly organized supplies, clear instructions, collections of natural objects, original art examples, and both books and reproductions of all types, the media centers provided rich opportunities for breadth and depth of learning. From that week on, students chose the ideas, themes, and materials they would work with, and made decisions akin to those of adult artists. As the teacher, I supported their explorations and capitalized on ways to make connections to art history, cultural topics, and new techniques. I also offered temporary specialized centers to provide more opportunities for students to explore a wider variety of media.

The curriculum combined independent work in the learning centers with a few select traditional lessons and was aligned with local visual art standards. In addition to materials and descriptions of helpful approaches, these centers offered an abundance of history and art appreciation materials that turned the entire art room into a learning center for visual aesthetics. The art classroom had transformed into a visual arts resource studio rather than just a place to pursue art activities (Joseph, 2002).

EMBEDDED ART HISTORY AND APPRECIATION

There are two ways to embed a visual resource studio with art history and art appreciation, through *indirect* and *direct* teaching. Indirect teaching uses the entire art room in the form of bulletin boards, wall displays, collections, and exhibits to expose students to visual stimuli. For direct teaching, these materials are organized to inform the introduction of new ideas and activities presented through teacher-directed discussions. Starting with indirect teaching, the rest of this chapter describes in detail a variety of approaches for introducing these art images.

Indirect Teaching

An art history time line, the type found in art education catalogues, is displayed along the upper part of the art room space. The timeline should be above the working area of the room but low enough for viewing by students. Some students will refer to this tool as their interests grow and will ask questions about its many aspects. The time line is also useful for direct teaching.

In addition to the time line, displays of individual artists' work and art movements can be set up to serve a variety of purposes. The culture and happenings in each school offer opportunities to create displays for student viewing. For example, if students are studying butterflies in their classroom, it is appropriate to create a related exhibit of mounted butterflies along with reproductions of art works that contain butterfly subjects. Flight and movement could also be emphasized with an ancillary exhibit that refers to these themes.

Subjects that students study are many and varied, from the culture of a particular geographical region to animals with backbones. Each could make an appearance as an indirect learning exhibit. Students who are studying these subjects arrive in the art classroom and immediately get excited about the exhibit. For the rest of the school population, these displays offer new ideas and images to contemplate or, for older students, the exhibits reinforce learning from previous years. Relating some exhibits to classroom learning not only augments the art classroom but gives self-directed students a chance to inform their art work with new insights.

An activity table in my art classroom contained a variety of stimulating materials that I had developed while working with Dr. Hurwitz. As an art teacher on his team, I created art history games and activities that helped children discern styles, identify artists, and understand their place in the continuum of human society. One popular activity featured mounted art reproductions from four very different art styles that were cut into puzzles of the same shapes. In order to do the puzzles, the student divided the pieces into piles of similar visual style. Included with the puzzle pieces was a list of questions for students to consider, such as "What word might you use to describe this particular style (for example, fuzzy, dreamy, floaty)?" Under the list of guiding questions were specific terms that the art world uses to describe these styles (i.e., abstract, impressionistic). Another teacher-designed game addressed the differences between the elements of art (the how of art making) and the principles of art (the why of artmaking). The choice of game subjects depends on the teacher's evaluation of which concepts need to be introduced and during what time in the school calendar.

A variety of commercially prepared games for use in the art classroom are available today, but teachers can create their own to speak to a particular concept that they deem important. The activity table also includes materials to enhance ideas that are introduced through the media centers. Special motivational collections have objects that can be removed from the table, taken to a student's workspace, and returned when finished. These are as varied as games using postcards to transparent color paddles that alter the spectrum of students' own work or a reproduction.

Small exhibits can be set up in the studio classroom to connect with children's interests. If a student or a group of students show an interest in a particular activity, such as creating interacting wire figures, that would be an appropriate time to set up a small Alexander Calder exhibit featuring books and reproductions of Calder's wire circus. If the teacher returns from a special museum field trip with gift store items focusing on a particular art-ist, those objects can instantly become a small indirect teaching exhibit. For instance, a collection of toy tin cars and airplanes highlights the interests of Andy Warhol, while a group of small African sculptures speaks to indi-vidual African cultures, as well as Pablo Picasso.

The Visual Resource Studio needs to contain a wide variety of motiva-tional materials and collections. Art teachers collect art books, postcards, and reproductions of all sorts. The school and local libraries are a useful resource and, of course, the Internet allows access to a world of resources. Students of all ages are influenced by these displays, and visiting classroom teachers will often find them both interesting and stimulating.

Direct Teaching

Along with materials and helpful instructions, media centers are em-bedded with multiple art history devices. Direct teaching is always used to introduce new media. As the whole class listens to the introduction of a media center, the teacher identifies and makes mention of these references. For example, the fiber arts center can feature reproductions of famous tap-estries, such as the French Bayeux Tapestry, along with real artifacts, such as Peruvian and Guatemalan weavings. Hands-on examples of weavings show how these influences can be used by the students to inform their own fiber arts work. Books highlighting contemporary fiber artists such as Jack Lenore Larsen and Navajo rug weavers expand student views of the range of fiber arts. When the teacher introduces the fiber arts center, these visual resources enrich discussions of each culture's contribution to the field. The studio classroom's time line can be highlighted at this time with each ex-ample placed at its historic location.

A word wall is very useful for presenting art vocabulary. Since it is a permanent display it would also be considered an indirect teaching tool, but it is most useful in its direct applications. As art vocabulary is introduced at centers, it is added to the art room word wall. Vocabulary relating to style such as realistic, abstract, and nonobjective is added as each term is introduced. The elements of line, color, form, shape, texture, space, and value; and the principles of balance, movement, emphasis, harmony, variety, rhythm, proportion, and unity can also be found on the word wall, along with groups of words to describe techniques. For example, the domain of printmaking includes relief techniques like wood or linoleum block as well as lithography and monoprinting. The differences between an original, a print, and a reproduction can also be added to the word wall. Important vocabulary is constantly being added by the teacher, who explains both its meaning and its connection to student work. Students are encouraged to enlarge their vocabulary by using these art words in conversation.

In centers-based pedagogy, direct teaching often takes place with an individual student or a small group. Because students are working on their own ideas and with their chosen materials, the teacher is freed up to relate to each student in an individual way. When a student creates something that speaks to the essence of a previous artist, the teacher can show that student how the work of each shares compatible concepts and approaches. If a student in the design center makes a piece using many squares in a variety of related colors, the teacher might say, "Look at what you are interested in!" Then, using reproductions, the teacher can show how the artist Vasarely was also interested in squares and colors. "This artist had similar interests as you. You are a relative of this artist in the family of artists." Vasarely could then be placed on the time line, and other "kissing cousin artists" such as Joseph Albers can be discussed. If a student draws a rather abstract collection of animals, a visit through reproductions and books to the Lascaux cave in France could prove fascinating. In this way, the time line is a helpful device to show when the cave paintings were created. When this kind of emergent teaching happens, other students often stop and listen and get ideas to incorporate into their work. We are, after all, a curious species—especially when we find subjects important to our own interests. In the learner-directed classroom, students' need to know arises when attention is paid to the intrinsic interests that the children themselves display.

ORGANIZATION

In order to have the flexibility to access such a large selection of artists and art movements, the teacher must continually keep these collections growing, organized, and readily available. A collection of labeled boxes containing smaller reproductions, with accompanying printed statements in the form of prompts and art examples, allows the teacher to pounce when the need for such materials arises. Along with the art boxes, a collection of hinged poster boards can be efficiently stored and ready to go. The boxes and hinged posters can be organized around both themes and artists.

Student interest is often the motivation to access this information, or a world event could be the reason, such as a solar eclipse prompting material on art references to the sky. Reproductions of English big wave paintings along with Japanese wave prints displayed in the aftermath of Hurricane Katrina show how artists respond to events in nature. After the devastating national experience of 9/11, a discussion took place in my classroom about symbols and the moment when a symbol, like a firefighter's badge, becomes an icon. The New York City firefighters' badge was a symbol that became an icon once it was infused with the emotion of 9/11. This sets the stage for a different discussion with students about graphic design. The work of such designers as Milton Glazer or product designers like Raymond Lowey illustrates other careers in the visual world of art.

The Visual Resource Studio housed a broad collection of books and catalogues. Art classrooms benefit from a diverse book collection, including illustrated general books on art, specific artists, and visual phenomena, augmented with age-appropriate books from museums. Of course, the Internet holds access to the entire world of art history and can be used as a resource by both students and teachers. With these varied resources, a dash to the bookshelves or computer will provide the teacher with just-right materials. When a student chooses to create a variety of clay sculptures on one subject, such as expressive animals, picking up a book on a sculptor such as Jacque Lipschitz allows the teacher to point out well-known artists who also had interest in interpreting animals. If a student pursues cartooning, books on well-known cartoonists, such as Charles M. Schulz, can be brought out. Young artists attracted to tissue collage could study Eric Carle's books. Students working with fields of watercolor can be shown work by Helen Frankenthaler, while children exploring shapes and lines can be exposed to Kandinsky and Miró. When students see that other artists traveled along a similar visual path, it helps them to more fully understand their own unique voice and the emotions that they bring to their own work.

Students finish their artwork at various times during a class. A book-listening area for young learners can be carved out of a small space within the art classroom. There, if students wish, they gather toward the end of class to see and hear a teacher-presented book. The books cover a wide variety of subjects about art and artists, or are chosen because of their illustrations. Discussions take place about the illustrations and how the illustrator achieved such visual imagery. If the book is an illustrated storybook, the teacher pauses in reading to ask how the artist gave the page a feeling of depth, or movement, or excitement. If a certain technique has recently been introduced in class, such as crayon resist, then reading a book illustrated with that technique is both exciting and important to the young student. Asking questions such as "How did this artist make this picture?" starts a class discussion that the students can inform from their own experiences.

Accessing these kinds of materials in spontaneous ways with individual students or in small groups is possible in an art room setting that encourages self-directed learning. A contemporary choice-based approach, such as Teaching for Artistic Behavior, allows teachers to attend to students' individual needs on a broad level and relate their students' investigations to any related segment of the art world. In order to nurture creativity, students must have the opportunity to work on what they are most passionate about, and come to know how related artists expressed their visual passions.

CONCLUSION

Over my 39 years as an educator, my career matured in unanticipated ways as the art program grew. Everything that I have stood for and believed entered into my teaching, empowering me with fluidity and flexibility. I could turn on a dime and respond visually to anything, both actual and virtual, that entered the classroom. When I had been a more traditional art teacher, I was tied to the constraints of a single lesson plan. The Visual Resource Studio proved to be far more exciting and challenging. Learner-directed practice freed me from overt discipline problems, organizing large quantities of identical materials, and making sure that students were following my directions. With those additional available moments, I could relate to students' interests and needs on a broader level, concentrating on the artwork of the human species. This pedagogy requires a delicate balance between intervention and restraint. Alert teachers can sense if they are intruding; if you know that you are *not* intruding, then you may go directly to the human spirit.

My centers-based art classroom was a laboratory that allowed students to explore and understand visual phenomena and how it affects the world. In addition to art materials and workspaces, it was essential that such a place be saturated with as much art history and art appreciation as I could provide. This gave my students the best possible chance to fully understand and inform their own explorations in creating visual images, brought alive through resources from the library, the Internet, and the art world. In return, my own teaching life became more aware and artistically rewarding.

REFERENCES

Barth, R. S. (1974). *Open education and the American school*. New York: Schocken Books.

Efland, A. D. (1990). *A history of art education: Intellectual and social currents in teaching the visual arts*. New York: Teachers College Press.

Gaitskell, C. D., & Hurwitz, A. (1970). *Children and their art: Methods for the elementary school*. New York: Harcourt, Brace & World.

Gross, R. (1971, September). From innovations to alternatives: A decade of change in education. *Phi Delta Kappan, 53*(1), 22–24.

Joseph, P. (2002). *Cabot Elementary School: Pauline Joseph's K–5 art class*. The Education Alliance at Brown University. Available at the Knowledge Loom site: http://knowledgeloom.org/practice_story.jsp?t=1&bpid=1360&storyid=1218 &aspect=1&location=3&parentid=1357&bpinterid=1357&spotlightid=1357

Part II

SUPPORTING LEARNER AUTONOMY

Stay back, observe, wait. It takes considerable restraint to allow for learning instead of stepping in and "teaching." Learning is most potent when it is a product of first-hand inquiry, exploration, and experimentation. Insightful teachers know this and trust their students to make mistakes, take risks, innovate, and reflect on both successes and failures. They provide their students the opportunity to discover information vital to their growth and development as learners and artists.

Authors in this part describe how, through discovery learning, their students unearth information vital to their growth and development. Placing students at the center of the learning experience means that teacher, curriculum, and space need to remain flexible in order to receive and accommodate the unknown directions taken by individual students with varying abilities, interests, and agendas. Cameron Sesto connects learner-directed pedagogy with Montessori methods in her chapter, "Building a Strong Voice of Inner Authority in a Montessori Choice-Based Art Program." Sesto's conviction that one essential role of the teacher is to provide nourishment for a child's developing inner voice causes her to consider every detail of her K–8 learning environment.

Tannis Longmore, in her chapter "Supporting Young Artists as Independent Creators," describes considerations for the very young child in a learning environment that supports curiosity and encourages risk-taking. Her keen understanding of the development of young children is evident in her careful attention to pace and well-considered classroom design. In this setting, safety and ease are featured such that even the youngest child can work with purpose and autonomy.

In his chapter "Testing the World Through Play and Art," George Szekely reminds readers that school is only a part of the child's world. This window into childhood passions and curiosities, as well as their competencies, illustrates that authentic learning is a collaborative venture between home and school. For the whole child to be present in school, teachers need to recognize and celebrate individual interests. Play, central to serious learning and inspiration, is vital for creative beings of all ages.

What percentage of a child's day at school is taken up by direct instruction and what part by experiential learning? How much of what is "taught" is learned? Teachers who create constructs for self-directed learning understand the value and impact of first-hand inquiry. Given what is known about teaching and learning, it is surprising that the models presented here are the exception rather than the norm.

Building a Strong Voice of Inner Authority in a Montessori Choice-Based Art Program

Cameron Sesto

A well-developed inner voice allows us to make healthy choices and decisions that enable us to live a life that provides spiritual nourishment as well as material rewards. It is our inner voice that allows us to say "no" when our peers are saying "yes" to reckless behavior. Or we can say "yes" to following a career path that doesn't fit into the accepted patterns of the day. This was the route that Jim Henson followed when he proposed making a living as a puppeteer. He created *The Muppet Show* and became one of the most widely known puppeteers in history. Possessing courage and the strength of conviction to do what is right for us in the actions we take and the dreams we follow takes many years to develop.

> Each of us has a wise part within, an intuitive part that knows what is true for us but unless this inner voice is carefully cultivated, we will forever be dependent upon someone else to provide the voice of authority. Learning how to listen to, connect with, and trust our inner voice are important skills—skills that need to be developed and strengthened slowly over many years. (Moorman, 2001, p. 51)

One of the best places to develop a child's inner voice of authority is in the art room working from original ideas. Making marks on paper and drawing pictures come naturally to small children. It makes sense that, through artwork, young children come to recognize they have meaningful ideas just like their parents, older siblings, and teachers. Children can learn to manifest ideas easily in both two- and three-dimensional work with materials such as colored pencils, crayons, clay, paint, or glue and sticks. Artist Georgia O'Keeffe (1976) observed that each of her paintings or drawings had been done according to one teacher or another, and then said to herself:

I have things in my head that are not like what anyone has taught me—shapes and ideas so near to me—so natural to my way of being and thinking that it hasn't occurred to me to put them down. I decided to start anew—strip away what I had been taught—to accept as true my own thinking . . . I began with charcoal and paper and decided not to use any color until it was impossible to do what I wanted to do in black and white. I believe it was June before I needed blue. (p. 44)

What then began to emerge and continue throughout O'Keeffe's life were the paintings that have become so admired and familiar to us all. If authentic artmaking is taught throughout the school years, it won't take 20 years to come to the realization that each and every one of us has unique ideas and creative ways of expressing those ideas.

How can teachers offer children content that will both increase their awareness of the world around them while making sure they also develop their inner world? Educator Maria Montessori (Cain, 2005), developer of the Montessori School movement, speaks to the design of an environment that supports the growth of the intellectual, social, and inner character of each young child:

Spontaneous activity in a prepared environment enables the child to follow his inner guide. Given freedom to follow the dictates of his inner guide, the child masters the physical environment, and constructs his intellect and social personality. This is reflected in the child's self-discipline and peaceful, productive attitude. Given freedom to pursue his interests, the child becomes self-directed in his learning and perseveres in tasks far beyond teacher assignments. (p. 19)

The Montessori teacher knows that children, like adult artists, have their own ways of seeing things. An inquisitive mind wants to learn and when curiosity has been aroused, the work at hand is a joy for both the artist and the child. The child may want to repeat a creation over and over again just like an adult artist will do. It's fun and it feels good to get better at something. When the artist senses progress, feelings of creativity and intrinsic motivation are at their highest (Pink, 2010).

THE MONTESSORI CLASSROOM

The Montessori classroom typically includes 3 grade levels of mixed-aged students working side by side. A classroom of mixed ages requires flexibility and the need to address diverse learning styles and abilities. Students learn from materials, their own research, exploration, experimentation, the teacher, and one another. Materials for learning are arranged in carefully organized areas, often displayed on two- or three-shelf bookshelves. Students learn to respect their work materials and put them away neatly for the next student to use. They may choose to begin the day with science and then do their math, or perhaps write a story in their journal. Teachers guide students into new areas periodically, leading them with new lessons when appropriate, based on observation of the student and his or her developmental needs. When children exercise their own discretion in choosing what to do and when to do their work, they develop self-discipline, a desire to learn, and the ability to concentrate.

Maria Montessori is known for her use of beautiful, well-crafted, self-correcting materials. For instance, in each Children's House Room for children ages 3 to 6, there is a bookshelf of materials dedicated to learning shapes. The triangle box is especially interesting since the box itself is made in the shape of a triangle with no top. Inside the shallow wooden box are several triangles of different angles that, when put together, become a large equilateral triangle. A thin black line is drawn on one or two sides of each colored triangles and when matched up, the shapes come together to make the larger shape. So simple, yet the child finds immediate satisfaction and success in putting the pieces together correctly. Along the way, the child learns about the angles in a triangle—right angles, obtuse angles, and acute angles. When students work with self-correcting materials, they also develop the ability to evaluate their results. There is no need to ask the teacher: "Is this right?" because the child can answer that question independently.

THE CHOICE-BASED ART PROGRAM IN A MONTESSORI SCHOOL

In the Montessori choice-based art room, areas or centers offering different media such as clay, paint, fiber, and construction supplies reflect the same purposeful arrangement of materials children are accustomed to in their classroom. In the art room, students listen to the art teacher describe a new technique or introduce a new medium in the same manner in which the Montessori teacher presents academic material. For example, the teacher may offer a lesson from the drawing center such as how to use hatching, cross-hatching, and burnishing with colored pencils. Students may choose to do this work and receive in-depth instruction during the class, or they may choose to work on their own ideas with the drawing materials. Others will delve into work in other centers. Many students express interest in trying the new work, and ask if it will be available at another time. Therefore, each new project or technique presented by the teacher remains available in the weeks to come for students to thoroughly explore at a later date.

In the choice-based art room, a 9-year-old happily constructs a dinosaur with newspaper and duct tape while a 6-year-old is busy painting a picture of sunflowers. One moment the teacher is showing two students how to use a wire armature to attach wings to clay birds, and the next minute she is in the fabric center showing one child how to sew using the blanket stitch. Next, she gives a longer lesson to a small group of students wishing to learn how to draw apples using the colored pencil techniques. When the teacher hears a student ask for help it is usually because the child needs one-on-one instruction, additional materials, or adult hands to help complete her idea: "How can I draw an eye so it looks more realistic?" or "Will you cut a door here in my cardboard?" The teacher encourages the development of students' original ideas and is a mentor for each child's artistic inquiry.

The choice of several media centers allows children to work in a manner similar to practicing artists. Some students spend months working in one medium and become deeply engaged exploring and fine-tuning their craftsmanship before experimenting with another medium. This approach most closely follows Montessori's ideas of freedom and interest. The children have autonomy to choose from personal interest, which can stem from their academic work, books they have read, family time, or a desire to learn a new technique or medium. Students are free to repeat and repeat, refining process and craft as they do in other areas of their lives. Children will then absorb a *knowing* of the medium that allows for experimentation and risk-taking without fear of failure. For example, I presented a "Creative Challenge" to a group of Lower Elementary students (ages 6 to 9) and asked if someone would accept the challenge to invent a stand that would hold a paper boat upright. A 3rd-grader with 3 years of experience working with construction materials immediately volunteered and, without sketching or asking the teacher any questions, took the boat to the table and set to work. By the end of the 50-minute class, a stand was created from wooden sticks and glue that held the boat in perfect balance. The boat stand designed by this child reveals creative thinking skills, an ability to visualize spatially, and self-confidence as well as an ability to determine when the work is complete. The student was able to tell classmates the successful step-by-step process and would be able to do so again if desired. This case demonstrates the power of experiential learning. It can be difficult to remember directions one has been told, but it is easy to repeat what one has discovered and internalized.

A CURRICULUM THAT STAYS CURRENT

Child-centered art rooms are alive with creative activity, an ebb and flow of nourishment for both the students and the teacher. Because of the variety of art being created, and the questions that organically arise as the work progresses, each art studio encounter contains unexpected moments of discovery, invention, and creative challenges. Students plunge deeply into their work, and the teacher moves from one area to another commenting, advising, and encouraging each student to reach their goal. Because the choice-based classroom is structured for individualized learning, the teacher has the opportunity to make specific and relevant comments about each student at assessment time. Using notes, photographs, and conversations with the children as well as observations of the development of the chosen work, the teacher observes and can comment on aspects such as: social interaction, fine motor skills, risk-taking, respect for materials, craftsmanship, focus, perseverance, and inventiveness, among others. Being able to comment on the whole child offers parents and administrators, as well as other faculty, a window into each child that would not otherwise be available. A child doing well in the art room may be struggling in other areas. A good report in art class may yield new teaching approaches for this particular student, based on information about the student's strengths and abilities within the art room.

Sometimes questions from an individual student offer teachable moments for the whole class. When talking about windows and transparency, the teacher holds up a piece of colored cellophane and asks the class: "Who can tell me if this piece of cellophane is transparent, translucent, or opaque?" In reference to an older student who is working on a landscape painting, the teacher may ask the class: "What colors can be used to make shadows instead of black?" An interesting discussion will ensue. When children have a deep desire to create, questions arise that the teacher cannot always know the answers to, so they turn to peers, the librarian, or the Internet for answers. "I don't know. How can we find out?" These are not uncommon words to hear from a teacher in a choice-based classroom. The student then understands that answers to questions can come from a variety of sources, not just the teacher.

In the choice-based art room there are never two classes exactly alike. This provides spontaneity and inventiveness in the workday for both student and teacher that often results in the sound of children singing while they are creating, and teachers who are eager to learn new techniques to help their young artists achieve their creative goals. Everyone wins when art time in school is a shared experience of interest, learning, caring, and creating for both teacher and student.

THE CONFIDENT HAND

A choice-based art room shows respect for the children and their choices. They inspire one another and, because the Montessori art class contains mixed ages, the older students often teach the younger ones and vice versa. Children learn to honor the diversity of expression apparent in work that leaves the art room—the seeds of respect for difference.

Young artists who engage in creative work are developing their inner resources of decision-making, critical thinking, and self-esteem. Because the student is so focused on the task at hand, there is great attention given to the work while watching how each step moves the artwork closer to the desired end result. Working in this manner, students learn to listen to their intuition. Self-discovery leading to the successful completion of a work of art (successful according to the student) offers the best platform for building self-confidence. If a student is unsure about the work, the teacher will hold the painting or print up away from the child and say, "When you step away from your work, you can see what it needs." The student invariably determines next steps and before long will not depend on an instructor or other outside authority figure for answers about personal creative work.

Confidence in one's abilities to assess artwork and make decisions about completeness is a necessary ingredient for building self-confidence and taking risks. Students working in the construction center make decisions about balance, stability, size, use of material, and function at each step of the construction process. Fine motor skills are taken to new levels of expertise when a 1st-grader sets to work with needle and thread intent on sewing a little pillow or a 2nd- grader makes a tiny boy from a circle and a star shape to add to a tree house. Better craftsmanship becomes apparent when fine motor skills improve, visible to the child as well as peers.

Whether building a submarine, painting a colorful picture, or inventing a cell phone from cardboard, young artists take great pride in their accomplishments and want to share what they have made with others. By sharing the work with classmates, children inspire other students to make similar work. They also become comfortable with their creative voice and gain confidence in what they believe they can accomplish. A strong sense of *self* develops when children invent projects that others also want to make. This in turn improves the student's technique and craftsmanship. Sharing creative work reinforces artistic confidence that comes naturally with the satisfaction and joy of creating authentic art. There isn't a manufactured toy in the world that can bring a child the same sense of pride, joy, and accomplishment.

TEACHING TO THE WHOLE CHILD

A choice-based art curriculum invites children to manifest their ideas within a cooperative environment. How and what children learn become apparent when observing students working for several years in a well-organized choice-based art environment with their peers. When the idea or the desire for creating artwork comes from the child, energy and passion pour into the work and the learning. The nourishment the child absorbs becomes visible through actions in the classroom as well as in the resulting artwork.

The teacher who offers a choice-based art program plays an important role in growing the character of each child. This mode of teaching speaks to the whole child and teaches from the inside out. "Character is not an item of knowledge which can be taught through learning or imitation. It is a conquest made during life through personal exercise and through personal experience" (Montessori, in Cain, 2005, p. 18).

It is as important to reach the heart as it is to stimulate the mind and train the hands. Intuitive decision-making and problem-solving within the artistic process build confidence in artistic skills and feelings of competence for the young child, and yield a strong voice of inner authority and high self-esteem. These qualities lead to a sense of great independence as well as a comfortable interdependence among the adults and peers in a young child's life. In a choice-based art program within a Montessori curriculum, children learn to think for themselves, take responsibility for their actions, and will eventually depend only on their own inner voices to provide guidance.

REFERENCES

Cain, R. (2005, Winter). Moral development in Montessori environments. *Montessori Life, 22*(4).

Moorman, C. (2001). *Spirit whisperers: Teachers who nourish a child's spirit.* Saginaw, MI: Chick Moorman and Personal Power Press.

O'Keeffe, G. (1976). *Georgia O'Keeffe.* New York: Viking.

Pink, D. (2010, March). *Drive: The surprising truth about what motivates us.* Keynote address presented at the annual conference of the American Montessori Society, Boston.

CHAPTER 6

Supporting Young Artists as Independent Creators

Tannis Longmore

Two painters stand at wall-mounted easels, brushing colors across large paper and onto their hands. At a low table, four children squeeze and pummel Play-Doh. Nearby, three toddlers tumble on a carpet-covered ramp, and two friends add to a long line of blocks. Happy companions pour water through funnels at a water table; a boy lolls on a cushion, closely studying the pages of a picture book; a girl flaps a yellow paper as she skips to a table set with baskets of crayons.

For the 2- and 3-year-olds in this cozy childcare room, art play weaves seamlessly into their day's work. Thoughtful adults have arranged a safe, attractive place for children to make discoveries about the world and their place in it, setting toys, art supplies, and books on open shelves and low tables so children can access them independently. A few limits keep things manageable, for instance: *paint stays at the easel; water stays in the water table.* Adults watch to ensure that materials stay out of mouths and converse with children. "How long your line of blocks is getting. Do you think it will reach all the way across the room?" "I see you are moving your crayon very fast round and round. Your red line goes around in a lot of loops on that yellow paper, doesn't it?"

TOWARD A CREATIVE CURRICULUM

Climbing down the big black steps of the school bus, facing the flung-open doors of school for the very first time, children's whole beings telegraph their feelings: awe, nervousness, fought-back tears. Real school. This place has been waiting for them, but have they been waiting for it? Some children approach eagerly; others hang back, tentative. Momentous things are inside that doorway: new experiences, unfamiliar rules, friends, conflicts, and sometimes, many compulsory, non-negotiable tasks.

Newly hired as art specialist at a public early elementary school, I would be introducing these 500 young children to the world of art and guiding several years of their artistic development. Providing time and materials to encourage spontaneous art play, as I had with my childcare charges, seemed an inadequate basis for curriculum in this setting, and so I created structured lessons. Designed to support children's creative growth within the framework of their current skills, using examples of art from history and around the world, these lessons would give students new scope for their own art. This was my plan, but as I worked with groups of youngsters for 1/2-hour and 50-minute stretches once a week, I felt that our work together was missing the *it* of art. The results were aesthetically pleasing and the children were generally content to complete my projects. But school art did not seem to relate to their spontaneous doodles at the edges of workbooks or their playground chalk drawings. My students were not truly connecting with the work. Instead of being absorbed into children's art, these lessons seemed layered over, obscuring where I meant to illuminate. Instead of getting to know the children through their art, I was managing projects. If the lessons were not supporting my students as independent creators, then what was the point? I needed to find a different way.

For an art teacher, as for students, the world of school is exciting but fraught with obligations: state and national standards, district curriculum, and, often, pointed comments about how a previous specialist approached art teaching. Attending to these while working with hundreds of children a week, art teachers, like our students, can feel swept up and hurried forward without pause to assess their surroundings or judge our direction. It is natural to reach for control. Teachers may worry that children will be confused or unruly if offered open-ended work. They may feel that an ability to direct children step-by-step to adult-pleasing products proves their value and worth, or that parents will expect their children to bring home pretty products. A series of directed lessons fitting neatly into the boxes of a graphic organizer, each with its own defined outcome relating to a particular Visual Arts Standard, or fulfilling this or that district curriculum goal, will be easy to explain to administrators. But what, exactly, are children learning about art, and about themselves as makers of art, through these contrived lessons?

Difficult as it can be to find time to look beneath the daily details, art teachers need to monitor the underlying messages of their teaching. Not understanding the developmental significance of scribbling and exploring, some teachers may feel uncomfortable with students' crayon scrawls and muddy, formless paintings, worrying that children are not being purposeful or may not advance. They may guide children to spend their time in art class assembling crafts or imitating art masters to achieve products recognizable to adults. If the main work of artists is to *not* follow directions to reach predetermined outcomes, then is it a legitimate way for beginning artists to spend their time? At best, it wastes children's time. Worse, it may foster dependency and lead to resentment, power struggles, and an erosion of the relationship between the adult and child. Worst of all would be if these activities superseded the children's natural creative drive, making them feel their own efforts were lacking and not worth doing. A hidden curriculum, opposite of the teacher's intention, emerges when all, or most, artistic and aesthetic direction comes from the teacher. In this unintended curriculum, creativity belongs to the teacher.

Knowledge of child development in art is the framework for educators to stand firm against imitation art and factory-assembly crafts. Understanding and recognizing the artistic stages children are growing through, from the starting place of markmaking and scribbling, helps adults to patiently support unfolding development with worthwhile creative experience.

For the youngest artists, the art studio is pared down to its essentials, and teachers will have to carefully choose which materials and experiences to include. Educators sometimes believe that young students need constant variety to keep them interested, since preschoolers generally work for a short span, have few skills, and little experience making art. But continual changes of media confine children to a stage of initial exploration with each, and students will have to depend on the teacher to tell them when, where, and how to work. Encountering different materials every art session can make the art room seem unpredictable and unsafe.

Instead, young learners benefit from opportunities to take initiative afforded by walking into their art room and knowing what to expect every time. A well-chosen variety of materials kept regularly available, with additional tools and techniques gradually introduced throughout the year, will ensure that there is something every child feels like working with each week, differentiating for varied working styles and attention spans. Young children construct knowledge of materials through repeated self-directed experiences. Students grow and change so quickly that they continually approach familiar materials with fresh concerns and abilities. Trust that children will challenge themselves at their own level—they will use their skills, ideas, and creativity to derive complexity from simple materials. Returning 4-year-olds in a 2-year pre-kindergarten program contentedly draw recognizable scenes next to the youngest 3-year-old scribbling for the first time. Through repeated use of media, young artists gain confidence and skills to create what they wish.

in the framework of familiar basic media, plan to introduce a ~~ount~~ of novelty—a new tool or a different size of paper—to the experience every couple of weeks, gradually enriching the studio choices. A sequence of painting experiences unfolding over the course of the year for pre-kindergarten might be painting initially with water, then with one tempera hue on shared paper, leading to an introduction of the routine for hand-washing. Next, children paint on their own paper, so that they learn where to choose a color of paper and how to place their painting on the rack to dry. Later in the year, children choose two paint colors to explore mixing hues. Finally, cardboard forms, like egg cartons and tubes, are added as choices of painting surface. A kindergarten class that experienced this sequence as preschoolers might be provided with water-soluble crayons for the first weeks, then with block tempera in primary colors, black, and white, along with a lesson on washing and drying the brush between colors. When most students are able to keep their palette colors clean, liquid tempera can be offered. Watch carefully for level of involvement—children happily engaged in discovering and enjoying the visual and tactile sensations of their work with materials are gaining a reservoir of skills and techniques to draw upon. Pacing is good when newly introduced materials, knowledge, or skills are being adopted into students' repertoires.

Young children are born scientists and artists, curiously experimenting on and constructing ideas about everything around them. They do not approach art materials with an intention to make a piece of art, a fear of not doing well, or otherwise limit themselves. They explore. Art and play are creative pursuits, connected with children's strongest feelings and desires. Lines scratched in dirt with a stick, blocks laid out in a pleasing pattern, a big smiling dot-eyed crayon loop floating on paper, trailing crooked legs beneath it—all these arise from within the child, and are their natural entry into the world of art. Educators must stay on the side of children and their creative growth. Children's art must be about children's ideas.

CREATING A STUDIO SETTING

Following their paraprofessional, a group of 20 3- and 4-year-olds sneaks into the art room. With a few small squabbles over space, they sit crisscross in a circle. Their art teacher joins them on the rug, acting surprised to see them and singing a call-and-response song with each child's name. A couple of children are feeling shy or obstinate, but most eagerly await their turn. "Today, the regular materials are open and we have one new thing," the teacher tells the children. Indicating the areas of the room, she continues,

"We have drawing at the table and on the chalkboard; Play-Doh; the cutting table with scissors and hole punches; puzzles; beads and sewing; and blocks here on the rug. The new thing today is painting with two colors, so we will go look at the painting table. Please stand up right where you are, put your hands behind your back and hold hands with yourself. Let's walk right over to look at the painting table without touching anything." As the children stand around the table, the teacher briefly describes and demonstrates routines. "When you paint, the first thing you need is a smock. You put it on like this. Today, I covered the whole table with big paper so we can do friendship painting. We can make enough room for everyone who wants to paint. You can pick up a brush and paint however you like on the paper. It is fine to put your brush into different colors. See, they mix." Pointing to art exemplar posters, she continues, "See all the paintings here on the wall? These artists loved to work with paint and mix their colors, too. Think about what kind of art you would like to create today. If you would like to work with Play-Doh, please walk to Play-Doh." As she names each material, children go to their desired tables; many get a smock and paint.

After only a few sessions, these students know the short routine that gets art class started. They know the materials that will be invitingly laid on tables. They move freely about the room, discovering the visual, tactile, and expressive qualities of each medium. Some create at one table for several weeks; others visit several different centers in one art session. Behind this smoothly functioning class lay many decisions and much preparation by the art teacher. Behavior guidelines, room layout, and media accessibility have been refined through trial, error, and observation of outcomes.

Many famous artists broke art traditions, societal norms, and even laws. Are rules and restrictions appropriate in a creative studio? Will lack of freedom inhibit children's exploration? Unlike an artist working alone in a studio creating as the mood strikes, school artists must operate on a set schedule, sharing materials and space. For many, these are challenging conditions. Opportunity for students to think and work independently must be balanced with the need for a calm teacher and an organized studio with sufficient materials for the many classes using the art room. Each situation will differ according to the particular school, room, schedule, group of students, and teacher's tolerance level. For example, will pouring and splattering paint be options? This is an enjoyable tactile, aesthetic experience, and a method employed by some working artists. In a room full of busy children, though, it could quickly become a safety and management issue, leading to overexcitement that could undermine the working atmosphere and frighten some children. The paint-pouring child could be gently given a choice, "You can make marks with your brush on the paper or you can pour water at the sink." Splattering could be a playground activity for warm days. Finding a way to say "yes" whenever possible protects children's sense of themselves as having lots of good ideas, while making it easier for students to accept the occasionally necessary firm "no."

Once rules are established, always assume breaches of expectations are accidental; work from a vantage point not of punishing misbehavior but of teaching that "this is the way we do things in art." When children are not being safe with materials or others, they stay by an adult who can temporarily stand in for the internal control the student has yet to develop or has lost in that moment. Simple guidelines, patiently taught and re-taught, will protect materials, keep children safe, and guide learners toward productive work.

Successful room arrangement facilitates independent, purposeful work. Details will vary in each teaching situation, but many teachers set up the room in centers, each focused on a single medium, with space for working, supplies, and varied art reproductions created in that media. The clear purpose for each center is revealed by the exemplars, materials, and what takes place there, so that children learn: *this area is for drawing; this place is for painting; here, I can build sculptures.* Further refining expectations for each center helps the studio to run smoothly. For example, if a teacher wants the expectation for the painting area to be: *here, we use a brush to apply colors,* then finger-painting experiences should happen in a different area, perhaps as a monoprinting experience. An inviting media center will include spaces for private, social, and collaborative work.

Easy access to supplies within each media center further supports children's autonomy. Fewer supplies are easier for children to keep in order; an overabundance of choices can overwhelm some children, and some young 3s will still be at the dumping stage. In art rooms used by older grades, pre-kindergarteners might be restricted to materials laid out on tables or on open shelves. Materials available to older children can be in closed closets or covered by curtains. At first, a few blocks and beads in each container may be enough; add more after a few weeks when the room is running smoothly. Shared or insufficient supplies can lead to grabbing and hoarding. Box lids can hold individual collections—a few crayons and colored pencils at the drawing table, or small selections of paper and fabric scraps at the gluing table. When children are allowed to bring an extra chair to a center where they want to work, they are less likely to shove a classmate aside. School life is full of opportunities to practice sharing: sharing space on the rug and in line, or sharing teacher attention. Providing plenty of space and materials for everyone in the art studio lets children get on with creative work without the frustration of waiting for tools and turns. Young children will proudly take responsibility for upkeep of the studio when it is manageable for them, making cleanup easy. Have defined places for everything and teach children where to get sponges or rags to wipe up smudges and spills.

A predictable art room with consistent routines, room arrangement, and materials helps children develop the feelings of security that they need before they will risk initiating creative activity. This is especially true for young children, for whom the process of separating from home and adjusting to school may, for a time, take all of their energy. If some hang back at first, remember that they are very little and there is no reason to rush them. Be friendly, but not overwhelming; talk about what you think they may be noticing; offer familiar and enticing materials; let them know it is okay to learn about the art room by watching. Trust that the growing familiarity and irresistible materials will be enough to eventually overcome reticence.

Children's autonomy is supported when adults in the art room calmly reinforce expectations, observe the children as they work, and respond with descriptive comments in ways that support children's intentionality. The comments may reflect the child's process: "I see you are moving your brush through the colors so they blend." Other comments will describe the product: "I see a lot of lines. Some are red, and some are blue." These comments support language learning, and small children appreciate the recognition and description of their activity. Children who are beginning to assign representative significance to work will likely volunteer further information, such as "I made my red and blue elephant." As children's thoughts and ideas emerge, take care not to impose adult assumptions. Announcing that a scribble resembles a butterfly is not respectful and can suggest that all artwork should be representational. Asking, "What is it?" forces the children to label their work, which may not be appropriate or desirable. "Tell me about your picture" is a more neutral approach with a reluctant child. Often, a descriptive comment, or simply looking at the work appreciatively, will prompt a young artist to talk about it.

The room is filled with a busy hum as clusters of children cut, paint, sculpt, stitch, and draw. While looking closely, showing initiative, and taking chances through creative work, students are learning that their peers also enjoy creating, that different people work differently, and that everyone needs space and friendly support. The teacher records the centers chosen by each child, watching and listening closely. Later she can reflect back to students what she sees them doing, helping them think about their process and learn words to describe their artwork. Children and teachers are getting to know one another as artists. Everyone in the setting is developing a sense of inclusion in a purposeful, enjoyable, creative learning community.

Five minutes have passed since the teacher turned off the lights briefly and announced, "Five more minutes for working in art class." Now, she flicks the lights again to say, "Stop your hands and your voice. When I turn on the lights, it will be cleanup time." As the lights go on, 20 momentarily stilled 3- and 4-year-olds spring back into action. Some begin to put things away, a couple dash across the room, several continue working on their art-work. After specific redirection from their teacher, "It's cleaning time, not creating time" and "I see you have a lot of energy. Can you use your strong muscles to go round and push in chairs?" The children soon have the room tidy and return to the rug. The teacher carries over the five or six drawings children have put in the Share and Take Home tray, and gathers students' attention with a finger play. As the work is handed out, each artist is invited to "Hold it in front of your stomach so we can see it. Do you want us to just look at it, or do you want to say some words about it?" Artists name colors they have used or tell what their artwork depicts. "When you finish sharing, lay your work on the rug, please." One boy rambles at length about his *Star Wars* picture, and the group is getting restless. The teacher gently intervenes: "Children are getting tired of sitting. Can you tell us one more detail and be done?"

Artists work by choice from their own vision, devising ways of inter-acting with materials to make that vision manifest. These little children, bumping up against one another in line, waving goodbye to their art teacher, are growing strong in the freedom to engage in authentic creativity. These children are artists.

CHAPTER 7

Testing the World Through Play and Art

George Szekely

The seemingly insignificant play acts of children are loaded with meaning. Momentary play, often annoying to adults, develops future notions of art. It is in play that a sense of design, taste, and art interests is born. Through play children begin to discover their future in art; they test potential tools, surfaces, and find new perspectives that sustain a lifetime of artmaking. Adults learn by observing children in acts of discovering art as they play in the school cafeteria, in a bathtub, or in their room. In directly observing children, art teachers can discover a timeless path for teaching art.

Artists of all ages explore the world through play and art. Acting on curiosity, children immerse themselves in firsthand exploration of their physical environment. Play is a means of interacting with objects and forms, testing materials, experiencing surfaces, and entering spaces. In play children create manageable models of the world so they can make modifications and restructure what exists. Playing allows for independent exploration and creates avenues to see things in fresh ways, to discover, and to invent. Play is a voice and a feeling that there is room for individual contributions to art and to restructuring the world.

Between play and art, play is the less recognized art form. Children themselves don't refer to the many acts of arranging, decorating, constructing set-ups, and tryout performances as art. Even though painting and drawing are called art, play continually challenges and opens up the notion of children's art to many yet to be officially recognized art forms. Children use play as a rehearsal for painting and drawing, and also as a way to independently discover new media. Familiar art tools and supplies expand the possibilities of play investigations and provide permanence to fleeting creative acts. Children's playful investigations and discoveries open new art ideas, ways of creating, practicing design, finding new art tools, and setting a foundation for imaginatively exploring things around them.

With play allowed and sparked in an art class, art is made through children's initiatives, in their way, and in their media. Play differentiates the art class from school. There are blocks, trains, teddy bears, and toys in an art class, some brought in by their caring owners, others made in class. There is movement, messiness, and noise, as everyone is not working in the same way, in the same place, on the same clock or time frame. Each art lesson begins with preliminary play that is a rehearsal for art, and sometimes the art itself. Preliminary play starts the art class with children's own investigation, separating their ideas from the teacher's plans. Each preliminary play leads to a thousand ideas for children. Each play contains the seeds of great ideas for further creations, constructions, paintings, and performances. As children grow up investigating through play, they bring this expertise to the art class. Children's play is not only their art, but also their means of discovery. Play is where art begins—in life and in an art class.

PLAYING WITH FOOD AND TESTING THE WORLD

A big no-no at home can give birth to major new art forms. Playing with food textures and colors, mixes and ingredients, becomes important color experiences, decorating trials, and canvas ideas. A child squeezing the season's first bright red cherries over a white napkin can explore paint marks and pit prints. An art class is a test kitchen that allows for messy beginnings and playful discoveries, and can be taken further into an art project. In the presence of sympathetic observers and enthusiastic helpers at home and in school, children recognize their own art in play discoveries. When children are taught the positive side of messes, and acquire the freedom to play with everything, they view art as intense experimentation and serious exploring. Into a fresh bowl of crusty cereal, a child places her elbow before the milk is poured. The act provokes immediate adult censure, a failure to understand a natural fascination with a mound of textures. The reasons for children's playful acts are often misunderstood, even alarming, and are often seen by adults as a challenge to decency and propriety. Yet adults need to acknowledge a child putting his face in a cup of applesauce to feel the cold texture. Many other unorthodox ways of experiencing materials and surfaces can be adapted to and furthered in art class experiences.

One of children's favorite art forms is preparing and decorating make-believe dishes of food. Art teachers can note and photograph children's many creative dishes, table settings, and restaurants, in which they turn pine needles and flower petals into food creations on white plates as canvases. Food experimenters pluck all kinds of objects from their ordinary existence and imbue them with food roles. Children set up restaurants and tea parties anywhere, and the environment becomes their vast art supply store. Adult artists can learn from children to make food out of vinyl, canvas, plaster, and concrete, and to possess a child's freedom in selecting art supplies.

CLIMBING AND SEEKING NEW VIEWS

Children look for various places to see the world in new ways. A young child with a stool is king of the world! A stool provides access to play with water in a sink, or satisfies a child's curiosity about the flow inside a toilet. A stool is a bridge to the mattress, a step stool to big chairs, and a ladder to kitchen drawers, just a short climb to the counter. High places, or "rooftop" views, fascinate children and promote the search for different perches from which to see the familiar. After becoming erect and moving from crawling on the floor, climbing is a large step in artistic investigation. Climbing allows getting closer to forbidden things and unfamiliar places. Children feel deeply satisfied when they are able to mount adult chairs on their own, and they will continue climbing to the table and to Everest, the highest points in a home.

An art room can be thought of in levels, having different heights on a topographical map. Art teachers may consider opportunities for students to tiptoe or step up or onto objects in classrooms. How can an art room be a field trip to higher ground and provide new views for students? Lifts can occur by raising the heights of shoes, or adding small crates, boxes, and pillows to climb as steps and hilltops to get a better view of things. Some flights and ascents are imaginary. The art room can be turned into an airport for magic carpets. Chairs can serve as gondolas for hot air balloons, or as launch pads for higher space adventures. A good story with some evocative gear and a playful setting can inspire art room climbers, pilots, and astronauts. Playful adventures are designed with student participation. Views from a parachute (umbrella) can be described in words or in pictures on the monitor of student-made cameras or cell phones. The search for fresh views is an essential aspect of making art, a constant exploration of new ways of seeing and finding new ways to interpret what is seen.

BOUNCING AND EXPLORING SURFACES

Adults admire the leaps of a ballet dancer, and marvel at the floor exercises of a gymnast or the turns of a figure skater, but may not yet be a fan of children as playful and inventive movers. One often hears adult remarks such as, "Why can't my kids just walk normally?" In school children are slowed, monitored, and stopped from moving as their searching bodies become silent and seated. Art teaching is about keeping the floors open to talented movers to rehearse and perform. An art room is a stage where students feel free to move again and to extend their movement with tools and toys. Feeling one's body move freely and playfully is necessary to giving life to an object or art material. Entering the art room can be pictured as an entrance to a dance studio. Art teachers who study children's dance, gymnastics, music, and movement classes, as well as all the playful movements in playgrounds and pools, find guidance to build a spirit of freely moving kids in an art class.

After conquering walking, children celebrate their freedom and move on to fancy walks, like bouncing, skipping, galloping, spinning, and walking sideways and backward. The desire to bounce and soar into the air, to spread wings, can be even more fun than climbing. Parents often find that any mattress becomes a launch pad or a trampoline. Bouncing to different heights, reaching imaginary targets, and jumping with a parachute (umbrella) can be part of art room playing. The desire to bounce and soar into the air, to spread wings, extends the fun in climbing. To bring the joy and feel of moving onto art surfaces, or the feel of dancing to working with art tools, sustains the life of action in art that is unique to children.

WANTED: PRIVATE PLAY SPACES

Young children call out "It's mine!" as others move into their territory. The clarification of ownership of objects and spaces is quickly corrected by well-meaning adults who encourage the virtues of sharing. While school is all about socialization, art needs to remain an area where things can be "mine," where children remain masters of their art papers, have complete jurisdiction over their canvas and art space, and art can remain their own. School teaches cooperation and team sports, but art needs to be a balance where children can protect their uniqueness and self-investment in ideas and objects, even if made in a shared and public studio. In an art room children are not asked to share everything or give up all of themselves. Art teachers insure that their students feel in control of material selections and all aspects of their artwork. Art satisfies a human need to work alone, to make things alone, to have and to keep what the artist has made. In art, room is made for the personal, and things are only public and shared if the art maker desires.

Children clearly define their possessions and territories. At home children know that this is my chair, my drawer, and my room! Even if they have their own rooms, children desire and gravitate to playing in and creating spaces elsewhere. Play and art in essence are the discovery and designation of one's own space and objects. When playing at home, children create their own classrooms to play school, and their own art studios and art tables to make art. Children love to explore and create their own stores and ballparks under tables, in closets, under beds, or in tents. A child wants his or her own closet or drawer so it can be specially filled and personally designed. A classroom is a public space, but in an art room art teachers consider the possibilities of privacy and ownership.

While having everyone sit to make art at rows of tables may help with crowd control, art teaching needs to consider variations in use of space. Tables may need to be set aside, even climbed under, to allow for more floor space. Instead of sitting on chairs, children may make play spaces behind them. Instead of working at tables children may play under them. Art rooms need boxes to play in, playhouses of all kinds. Suitcases, pocketbooks, and lunch boxes can be private art worlds to be designed, carried, and closed for privacy. As children explore the world they need a home base to return to with their sightings and findings to be thought through and acted upon later.

TESTING OBJECTS BY PLAYING AND ANIMATION

The story of figurative sculpture in children's art is intertwined with a child's relationships with figurative objects such as dolls and action figures, and their ability to animate these inanimate objects, bringing the figures to life. Through play, children's relationships with play figures evolve and change. The special relationships children have with their dolls and teddy bears is partly a development of animation, and of course the development of love, attachment, and caring for others. In playing with their "babies," children not only become aware of the figure in sculpture but how figures are made to portray people—themselves and their family. In experiences with animation, they learn to act out their own life, their hopes and fears. They learn to animate baby to take a nap, dress up, and arrange the figure in multiple backgrounds and settings. Children form an early attachment to figurative sculptures. They love the figures they animate, an idea that is useful to understand in teaching art.

"Where is my baby?" means where is my faithful friend who shares my life, goes everywhere with me, and tests my world? Through playing with baby, children receive exceptional theatrical training, learn to hold the figure, create poses, expressions, and lend sounds and voices to them. All kinds of artwork can be made for play friends: clothes from paper towels, beds from boxes, and pillows. A new repertoire of movements is added. Young sculptors always carry their models with them. They look to the outside world for new scripts, scenarios, and story ideas. As the child's movements become more sophisticated, so does the dolls'; the child's figure-handling skills grow. Baby's discoveries relate to the child's discovery of the body and its moves. By the time children begin school they enter as skilled performers, ready to pose any figure and animate any object in the art class.

The attachment to figures and the adventures of animating and directing them reaches well into the school years as it continues with animation of action figures, fast food figures, little ponies, robots, and so forth. As animators develop more trained hands, their figures may get smaller. As the child becomes more worldly and verbal, their figure set-ups reach into larger groupings and casts with more elaborate settings and staging. Their animation art comes to include fantastic and more complex stories. The stars of a show are no longer babies or the self. As children become worldly so do their characters, coming from movies, video games, and other planets. As children engage in life outside the home and discover more imaginary places, their foot soldiers become dinosaurs and interplanetary adventurers. It is not uncommon to find unusual backdrops for performances, and to light the show with home lighting discoveries. A study of the history of play figures, for example early toy dolls and immobile soldiers made from ceramics, tin, and plaster, leads to comparisons with today's plastic sculptures that have complete freedom of moving, bending, and posing.

Today "home theater" means having a large flat-screen television with multiple speakers. For children it can mean the many performances they put on for family and guests. A great deal of children's playing is performance art in which they star. Performance art is children's great art form, which inspired adult interest in performance art. To fully appreciate students as veterans of show business and performance art, art teachers can attend and even participate in children's home theater productions. What children learn from performing in an art class is that art can be about adding oneself to the object world, providing not just movement and voices to any figure, but investing art with oneself. In a performance, all objects can talk, be played with, and have many lives. Children also learn that art is working with an audience that ultimately responds to one's art. And yes, clapping is encouraged in the art class. Artists often don't get the applause needed to encourage their art.

TESTING THE WORLD BY WEARING EVERYTHING

Build-A-Bear is one of the fastest-growing mall chain stores. Children pick their teddy bears from a dozen available models and watch the teddy bear being "born" or stuffed and dressed in the outfit of their choosing. While building your own suggests creativity, there are few choices to be made in the bear. Yet children start their play experimentation by dressing scores of play figures and wanting to choose their dolls and their own clothes. Picking out their own clothes at age 2 is part of a creative yearning and an early start in exploring fashion arts. In doing so, children are making personal and artistic choices in style, color, and fabrics. Children who are active in dress-up play will dress up their pencils and pets, wrap a plaster outdoor deer in jump ropes, and cover its antlers with badminton birdies. Children explore sculpture by wearing it, putting on an unusual found container, trying on hats, or modeling baby blankets. Before children learn to make masks in school, they have tried on many objects, covered themselves in many materials, wrapped themselves in foil and paper towels, and invented clothing and masks from everything at hand.

Art is encouraging freedom in expression and allowing a reprieve from standard fashion rules and adult dictates such as matching "appropriate colors." Art teachers become experts in children's costumes and dress-up play, using the art class to further their efforts to make their own clothing and wardrobe choices. Art class can have regularly stocked fabric trunks, dress-up corners with mirrors, and opportunities to make and try clothing on resident play figures. Designing art ideas related to the body is similar to choices made over other canvases. Art class is the place where a child builds his or her own bear, makes its own outfits to explore fabric colors and patterns, and tries on everything as a way to test objects and art ideas.

TESTING THE WORLD BY FIXING IT

A child walks over with a marker and exclaims, "I broke it!" Seeing the inkwell and bright red color drippings, the adult is unsure if it was an accident. Nevertheless, it's clear there is great interest to discover what is inside the marker. Before getting angry adults have to step back to consider what children learn from an experience. Children explore objects by taking them apart and seeing how they work. Before labeling a child destructive, the need in artistic learning for dissecting, looking inside, and even breaking something that works to gain access to its parts has to be considered. Sometimes it takes a screwdriver or even a hammer for a young artist to investigate. Teaching art is about encouraging playful looks at exterior surfaces and views, but also allowing for going inside and pursuing the mysteries that lie beneath the skin of a worm or the locked interior of an alarm clock.

To be a sculptor is to admire engineering and the beauty of interior structures and mechanical parts. Art teachers stock up on old typewriters, phones, and alarm clocks from second-hand stores. All children need a toolbox and an art room to use it in; they need to fix things by taking them apart, and boxes to collect parts in. Tool belts are exciting for playful investigators. There can be many opportunities to save, sort, and trade parts, showcasing and arranging them in see-through containers. Operation is an art game of basic sculptural fantasy, of pulling parts from the inside of things to appreciation the forms and their workings. Assembling and disassembling, constructing and destructing are important acts in building artworks in any medium.

The familiar building and kicking over of blocks to experience the fall is a basic play act and a valuable art study. Children are not destructive in turning things upside down. Dumping things from the inside out allows them to see how objects fall–an important learning experience for architects, sculptors, and engineers. Surgical masks, scissors, and tweezers promote operating and dissecting in an art room. The "patient" may be an apple or an old cell phone. Old artworks may need fixing, and artworks in progress are always in need of repair. Art teachers can create opportunities for children to see the nature of art as something that is continually being built and sometimes taken apart.

TESTING SURFACES BY SPREADING AND DUMPING OVER THEM

Children are frequently accused of making messes. The spread of marbles on the floor or cereal on tables is difficult to condone, yet the freedom of dumping out a container of candies, toothpicks, or marbles over carpets or floors becomes a visual feast that children learn from and use for a lifetime of artmaking. Art is an act of freely spreading objects over different surfaces.

Creating purposeful accidents is a valuable tool for testing relationships, positioning of parts, and, later, constructing visual relationships in the puzzles of art. Spilling things seems like an undesirable play act. Children enjoy dumping the contents of packages both as an act of celebrating freedom as artists, and also as a way to follow the paths of the parts. They notice the sounds of falling objects and the way the spreading objects assemble themselves on a carpet or grass. For adults it is a matter of who will pick things up, and they often don't stop to admire the result. In fact a great deal of contemporary art pays homage to children's playful ways of spreading and pouring. Recognition of children's funny and unusual ways of studying art and design results in the creation of controlled classroom opportunities for practice.

Children could just take things one by one out of a toy box, so why do they dump them all out at once? Because dumping is a creative act that creates a wealth of ideas; it creates a visual variety, rich in possibilities that taking things out one at a time does not provide. Dumping is an idea starter, a way for children to fill surfaces and canvases and then observe the results, providing ideas for organizing, selecting, and starting to build a painting or a sculptural form. Spreading and dispersing is a way for children to shake up views and move objects around.

Dumping play comes to be closely tied to cleanup play. After dumping all the marbles from a jar, the child is asked to clean them up. The cleanup is a slow process, as the child invents creative approaches. Some marbles drop into the child's curly hair and then roll into the jar by a tilt of the head. A handful of marbles are placed into the cap and rolled into the jar after being rotated in the lid. This, like other cleanup tasks, which children are required to do, can be expected to be slow because children undertake them as opportunities for invention and making art with a new medium. After seeing the marbles all over the room, and waiting for them to be gathered back in the jar, the parent says, "These marbles won't come out again till you're 30!"

There is a similar dilemma in school—some teachers, like many parents, prefer neatness and see dumping and pouring as destructive acts and as a defiance of order and rules. But as art teachers learn to organize the art room so paint spills will not cause a problem, there are many fabrics with mesh and holes, containers with rims, bumpers, and framing edges that allow all kinds of pickup sticks to fall and marbles to roll. Playing inside a play pool, pizza box, pizza tray, or hula hoop allows for active pouring, dumping, and spreading.

TESTING OBJECTS AND SPACES BY CRAWLING UNDER AND INSIDE THINGS

Fix-it artists want to peek inside objects, but many children also crawl to get inside containers, spaces, and furnishings with their bodies and imaginations. These are young artists who seek out private studios, and design their own play spaces inside containers or behind or under furnishings. When walking through the curved steel walls of a contemporary sculpture in a museum, one is reminded how adult artists learn from and expound upon their experiences of climbing into and walking through spaces and containers they found and made as children. My family's summer weekends are special because our neighbor comes up to the mountains with a big white cooler, bringing the best delicacies that New York delis have to offer. The children wait patiently for the Styrofoam containers that they quickly lay claim to, and rapidly move indoors to remodel. One week the cooler becomes a race car, the next week, a speedboat, and after several weeks the coolers are coupled to become a circus train carrying the children and their stuffed animals. As a child, the laundry basket was my fort and clubhouse. Children will quickly claim any large container that arrives in a home or art room.

Children often play and enjoy exploring the darkness and privacy of caves or theaters set up under the kitchen or dining room table. Activities under a rolltop desk can vary from a baseball stadium to a vast underground garage. Closets are designated as private play spaces, and refurbished for playing school or as an art studio. It would take a book just to describe all the things that have been created by children who entered kitchen cabinets.

Outdoors, children are masters at spotting openings in a bush to envision a playhouse inside. What is life under the art room table like? What is inspiring about playing under a grouping of tables? How can children's investigation of spaces be continued and enhanced in the art class? Art teachers can help students to drape tents over tables or suspend blankets between chairs. Interesting containers and spaces speak to kids, inviting them to envision playful uses and providing comfortable interiors. The value of experiencing different spaces and testing their feel and volume in relation to their bodies prepares children for dealing with the problems of space in all art forms.

Getting into laundry baskets or trash cans can be a lesson in experiencing and envisioning forms from the inside. Transforming and furnishing space is an essential quality to preserve in children as future designers, architects, sculptors, or painters. Before space is abstracted or flattened in artworks, young artists need to be encouraged to sleep in it, feel it, squeeze into it, and playfully explore it as their art.

SUPPLIES TO TEST THE WORLD

Children's creative supplies are not limited to traditional art supplies. Each supply children frequently play with can be considered an art supply to be explored in the art class.

Water

Water is a child's most basic art supply. Playing in a bathtub studio or at the beach provides investigations in pouring, funnelling, straining, soaking, and also allows children to study drips, experiment with waves, create waterfalls, or play with bubbles. School paints are wet, flowing water and colors. Experienced water players exhibit a free painting spirit. Water play conducted in the art room enhances painting experiments and ideas. Instead of a sink or the bathtub, an art room can substitute trays, play pools, and funnels to explore playing with water and colors. Color can be added to wet sponges, squeegees, hoses, and basters to animate water in tubs as students perform on soft canvases and various papers. The ways children play at the sink and at bathtime provide inspiration for art room water-play sites.

Glue

Children pour, scribble, and freely draw with glue. They pour glue from containers, through their fingers, on their hands, and playfully make circles on any surface. Children put their hands and heart into glue playing, making glue sandwiches by attaching papers with surprise inserts. The slimy, sticky surfaces are an artistic way to join all kinds of household objects. For many adults it's just a waste of glue and paper, instead of children's poetry. They desperately try to intervene, teaching children how to use the glue correctly instead of encouraging an important inventive act. Children learn that they can join any form to any other form, that leaves can be joined with candy wrappers to make art. Bottles of glue promote playful scribbling and drawings and the fluid joining of objects stuck together like flypaper. Adding color to white glue or enlisting new dispensers are ways school art can expand glue play.

Tape

At home tape is everywhere, yet never a fresh roll to be found. Young children acquire artistic power from being able to use a tape dispenser and by displaying anything, anywhere around the home. The discovery of tape is a big art and design step, as things start to be taped over doors and windows, as children discover the many available home canvases besides the refrigerator. Tape becomes spider nets suspended around the home, providing a creative way to join and wrap any object. Tape makes all children's art wearable and leads to a love of all kinds of sticky decorating, like covering bodies in Band-Aids or stickers. Art teachers are sensitive to children's art material interests and their preferences for materials that have playful qualities. The most important children's materials may not be in art supply stores or catalogues; they may have to be gathered by everyone in class.

Play-Doh

Play-Doh can be shaped into any play food or take on the appearance of any play figure friend. Play-Doh demonstrates the need for flexibility and instant reshaping necessary in children's play supplies. Play-Doh and other flexible supplies are important for art class warm-up or preliminary play and idea-gathering tasks. The malleability of children's favorite play materials allows for an assembly line of instant noses, rows of action figures, or snack food ideas to be constructed before anything is drawn or painted. Play-Doh can lift any surface impression, and becomes an instant explanation of texture or even helps to illustrate printmaking. Like tape and glue and other good experimental supplies, Play-Doh is sticky. When they apply it to any large ball, children come up with a variety of faces, imaginary planets, and globes.

Aluminum Foil

Foil is another favorite experimental children's supply, and has the flexibility of Play-Doh. It is a flexible skin, instead of a flexible form. Many children's art forms of wrapping are found in foil play, such as creative approaches to diapering dolls and covering them in baby blankets or space clothing. Children experiment with new fashion trends, creatively wrapping themselves in foil. Children discover that aluminum foil instantly duplicates any toy, and when rubbed against any natural surface it naturally lifts off the most delicate print. In adult terms, wrapping or covering forms leads to a deeper understanding of them, just as when waxing a car one discovers subtle curves and details. A testimony to children's interest in the magical qualities of foil is that there is never enough of it at home, so that plastic wrap is often substituted. Wrapping is an early sculpture act with magical qualities—now you see it, now you don't. It clarifies and abstracts forms by providing a cover and a new canvas to decorate. Tape, stickers, Play-Doh, and plastic wrap all possess similar magic.

Makeup

Everyone fondly recalls touching noses, squeezing cheeks, and pressing up against each other's faces as children. Learning to name parts of the face is assisted by fun games. The many loving kisses on the nose or forehead are early facial explorations. Peek-a-boos practice facial recognition, similar to the discovery of one's face in the mirror, and are part of the education of portrait artists. Children like to style their own hair and decorate it with ornaments. No wonder in many children's drawings there is such attention paid to hair. Through play, children fine-tune portrait knowledge and an interest in exploring the face. When portraits are revisited in the art class, art teachers need to be aware of the playful and loving journeys that started with makeup play and face painting, and not just concentrate on formulas for drawing faces. To continue an interest in the subject, the ways and means of approaching portraiture need to remain fun and playful, with constant references to face painting, reminders of the joys of playing with mom's makeup, trying on stickers or hats, and other fun ways to look at and alter one's image.

fun day?

INVENTING PLAY

Children explore their world by inventing new rules for playing. This is especially evident in the way children make up their own rules for traditional games. For example, an adult works with a young helper to set up a croquet field. After the game pieces are laid out on the lawn, there is a period of explanation and demonstrations of how the game is played. When play is about to begin, the child says, "I know a better game!" She vividly describes her vision of playing croquet using two mallets instead of one, striking two balls simultaneously. Not yet sanctioned by the United States Croquet Federation, nevertheless the stakes are reset in a circle, with participants putting from the middle of the field. And so it is for playing table tennis under instead of on top of the table, or playing chess on a board set up by a child as a royal marriage ceremony. Children change the rules, and art teachers need to step aside.

Children also change the "rules" of adult artmaking, or as adults perceive and sometimes teach art to children. In art class teachers can use vivid examples and tell stories of children inventing games in a swimming pool or on the croquet field as an artistic act. Children in an art class can invent board games or redesign field games as a demonstration of how art is about changing the rules of the game and discovering one's own game plans for solving art problems.

CONCLUSION

Playing is a happy occasion, and that is why so much of children's play deals with parties and celebrations. Through playing children build and maintain all the essential ingredients for making art, especially the joy in artmaking. Parties, performances, pretending, and playing in an art class maintain the unique qualities that characterize children's art. Children's joyful playing is a means of investigating the world, and a way to begin shaping creative responses to it. Studying and taking seriously children's playful activities outside of school are important in deciding on approaches to art teaching.

Most important, in playing, children in an art class become children again. Playing gives art back to the experts—children, who are comfortable and familiar with this art form. Players don't feel like they are in school; they are free to investigate, set up, search for their own ideas. Play moves children out of school, in body and spirit, in attitudes and actions. As players, children lead the art class, creating non-school moods, moves, and frames of mind that allow children to pursue a child's art.

Part III

SPECIAL CONSIDERATIONS FOR SPECIAL POPULATIONS

Special populations, with out-of-the-ordinary needs or interests, flourish in student-directed programs where artistic license is granted in a construct of inclusion. Marginalized, disenfranchised students find that it is safe to voice and explore unconventional ideas and approaches. Students who are gifted and talented and those with disabilities are elegantly and easily accommodated by self-adjusting environments where the expectation is that everyone works in his or her own way. Boys, whose interests and very nature can be stifled or even shunned in school, discover a place to explore subjects that are commonly taboo in school. Preadolescents, a group that demands recognition in its own right, require and receive the right balance of freedom and support to help them in their search for identity and relevance.

Students with deep passions and unusual interests finally find a positive environment for the development and expression of ideas in choice-based settings, as evidenced by Nan Hathaway's description of highly creative, nonconforming students in "Outlaws, Rebels, and Rogues: Creative Underachievers." Here, authentic learner-differentiated curriculum assures that every learner can work from individual strengths and interests. Ilona Szekely examines the perplexing developmental stage of preadolescence in "Look in the Mirror: Reflecting on Middle School Art." Szekely validates influences of home and popular culture in emergent curriculum for middle school students wrestling with self-image and peer influence. The action of transferring ownership to the student is transformative for both teacher and learner. Ellyn Gaspardi describes how learner-directed programs are naturally accommodating for students challenged with learning differences and special needs in "Teaching for Innovation: Supporting Diverse Learning Communities." This confirms the powerful impact of relationships and trust in the learning community. These convictions are tested in "The Secret Art of Boys" by Clyde Gaw, which addresses the social and emotional development of boys in the post-Columbine climate of fear.

Teachers who encourage students to self-direct exhibit a high level of acceptance and trust. Such teachers demonstrate the courage to champion the rights of children.

CHAPTER 8

Outlaws, Rebels, and Rogues

Creative Underachievers

Nan E. Hathaway

You know the type—the outlaws and rogues who seem hell-bent on breaking rules and demanding attention. Hats left on inside the building, loud and late for class, iPod earbuds dangling, and plaid boxer shorts jauntily displayed above their jeans; they challenge authority at every opportunity. These charismatic leaders hold court in your classroom and preside over their admirers. They get tossed out of French class, and have a reserved seat in the principal's office. Their grades are awful but they are bright—sometimes extraordinarily so. Parents and teachers agree that they are not performing to their full potential.

How about this rebel—does he sound familiar? Labeled dyslexic or ADD/ADHD (Attention Deficit Disorder, Attention Deficit Hyperactivity Disorder), this student refuses to open a book or pick up a pencil. Homework is out of the question. He won't take notes and his handwriting is illegible anyway. During class discussions, however, this student commands the floor. He has opinions on novels he never read and theories about subjects that have not been introduced. His vocabulary outmatches the teacher's, and he is teaching himself to play the guitar. He knows and can diagram every constellation in the galaxy (and beyond), can list what Cleopatra liked for breakfast, and identifies birds by ear. He scores in the 99th percentile on standardized achievement tests and is failing every subject.

Here's another, an outlier; do you know this student? She is heavily armored under an oversized hoodie or protected behind long bangs. It is the 3rd week of school and you have not yet heard her voice. Her hair color has already changed twice. She sits by herself and draws on her hands. She carries around a journal filled with sketches and poems and works on these in math and science, when she is supposed to be focused on classwork.

And then there are the outcasts. You know these kids, too. They wear sweatpants and screened tee shirts—the elastic waist is more comfortable than jeans, and the image on the shirt depicts wolves or dolphins, other endangered species to which these kids relate. The labels have been removed from inside their clothing because they itch. Sock seams are irritating, too. With nose in a book at recess and at lunch, this student dons a different sort of armor against tormentors. More comfortable conversing with adults than mixing it up with peers, brainy kids are teased or shunned, unless teams are forming for the geography bee.

If anyone ever checked, many of these students would score in the gifted range on standard intelligence tests. Most teachers and administrators, however, have received little or no training in gifted education, and don't realize that the incorrigible behaviors they sometimes battle against are common in gifted individuals, and that creativity is a trait strongly associated with giftedness. It turns out that the rebels, outlaws, and rogues in school form a group worthy of close examination when farming for hidden talent. Many gifted kids are convinced there is something wrong with them and don't know that what's "wrong" is that they are gifted and creative (Silverman, 1993). Understanding the lesser-known traits associated with gifted kids can help to clarify why they are often at odds with their teachers and others at school (Davis, 1999). This knowledge can be leveraged when designing appropriate programming for this population.

Nonconforming, rebellious, and self-sufficient, these students may also be courageous and protest vigorously at perceived injustices (on behalf of both themselves and others). Gifted, creative students may also appear impatient and demonstrate a low frustration tolerance, and be excitable, impulsive, outspoken, and persuasive. Gifted individuals may struggle with perfectionism or be forgetful and uninterested in details. Dismissed as immature or temperamental, compulsive or strong-willed, coddled or spoiled; gifted, creative kids usually stand out one way or another. Sensitive, confused, and misunderstood, they strike out or shrink within themselves; teachers lay down the law and parents throw up their hands. These *creative underachievers* are often underidentified, misunderstood, and underserved. These students possess an internal locus of control, a trait that sometimes sabotages their willingness to follow step-by-step directions or other school conventions. Many creative but at-risk students fail to thrive, even in programs specifically designed for gifted students.

Addressing the unique needs of highly creative but unsuccessful and often marginalized gifted students is a challenging undertaking. Teachers are often surprisingly poor at recognizing students who are gifted, more often nominating "teacher-pleasers" who are polite, willing, and hardworking for gifted programming (Davis & Rimm, 2004). Many underachieving students are never tested or identified as gifted—to the contrary, their attitude and performance in school convince teachers that they are more in need of re-mediation or discipline than acceleration or enrichment. These youngsters are experts at challenging authority, dodging rules, and setting their own agenda, behaviors that rarely endear them to school faculty who may be the gatekeepers for entry into higher-level classes. In some cases, it is assumed that gifted kids already have an advantage over their peers and so don't merit specialized programming. The idea is that because of their giftedness, they will do just fine without any extra support. Unfortunately, creative students expected to conform to traditional school norms often drop out, both literally and figuratively.

It is interesting to note that the most creative kids probably are not the ones with the highest IQ scores. Instead, the highly creative ones typically fall in the marginally or moderately gifted range, not much above usual cut-offs for gifted programming (Betts & Kercher, 1999; Davis & Rimm, 2004). So, the fact is that the behaviors and traits that could signal creativity and giftedness more often irritate and challenge teachers, and result in a school career peppered with power struggles, detentions, failure, and lost potential. Creative students may become marginalized, angry, or self-defeated due to school norms that underscore students' deficits and disregard their creativ-ity. Given the current focus on remediation over the practice of teaching to strengths, the unique abilities of our most creative youth may be suppressed well into adulthood (Robinson, Shore, & Enersen, 2007).

SCHOOL NORMS THAT SUPPRESS CREATIVITY

I come to school each day with all these ideas in my head and no place to paint them. (6-year-old boy)

Creativity, which should be celebrated as an asset, is instead a hindrance at school. Sir Ken Robinson (2006, 2010), a renowned expert on creativity, asserts that the longer children attend school, the less creative they become. Schools systematically stifle creativity, and place value instead on compli-ance and convention. The almost endless routines and customs of schooling consistently work against highly creative children, pit them against author-ity, and inhibit original thinking and action. Desks in rows, assigned seat-ing, short class periods, prescribed curricula, frequent transitions, pacing to meet the middle, and a focus on extrinsic motivation (grades, behavior charts, and rewards) limit creativity and marginalize creative individuals. Teachers, tethered to lesson plans, may be resistant to tangential questions, especially in an era where students are required to demonstrate proficiency (and not much more) on high-stakes tests. Teachers are accustomed to determining content, process, pace, and product for their students, and may resent sharing this role with self-directed learners. Highly creative children, faced with these conditions and expectations, may apply their considerable talents to evade work, disregard rules, and torment their teachers and school administration.

Yet gifted, creative children are learning machines! These students typically display intense interests and passions, possess considerable idiosyncratic knowledge, and demonstrate the ability to maintain prolonged focus on topics of interest. They exhibit tolerance for ambiguity, attraction to complexity, a sense of humor, preference for discovery learning, experimentation, exploration, and the alertness and ability to capitalize on serendipity (Colangelo & Davis, 2003; Davis, 1999; Davis & Rimm, 2004). These kids learn best when afforded flexible use of time and the chance to incubate ideas. In school, creative youngsters find that the expectation is for them to comply and perform on demand—habits that improve success in school but undermine creative potential (Hartmann, 2000; Robinson, 2006). In some instances, "teachers may structure learning experiences to reduce creativity because they do not value creative thinking and find it difficult and time consuming to evaluate" (Robinson et al., 2007, p. 82). Students who refuse to conform to teacher demands and expectations are relegated to a desk in the corner or private seating in the hall. They may also be remediated, medicated, and subject to endless, degrading behavior modification plans.

CONCEALED POTENTIAL

Thousands of geniuses live and die undiscovered—either by themselves or others. (Twain, 2000, p. 181)

In addition to the already confounding personality traits associated with this population, various other characteristics and conditions can be at play with highly creative, underachieving students that can obscure ability and conceal potential.

Asynchrony

Asynchrony, or uneven development, is a hallmark for gifted, creative children. It is common to find that children with exceptional cognitive abilities experience relative weaknesses in other areas of their development. Asynchrony may manifest as unusually immature social behavior in combination with accelerated academic capability, or 9th-grade reading ability combined with 1st-grade penmanship.

Twice Exceptional

While uneven development in gifted children is the norm rather than the exception, some children may be identified as both gifted and disabled. Referred to as *twice exceptional,* these students might not be identified for gifted programming at all because their disabilities mask their gifts. Tragically for this group, their gifts may also disguise their disabilities, so that neither gifted programming nor remedial academic support is offered. Twice-exceptional children may appear "average" on test scores, yet they are anything but (Davis & Rimm, 2004; Robinson, Shore, & Enersen, 2007; Torrance, 2004; Winnebrenner, 2000). Graphs of subtest scores on standard intelligence tests for children who are twice exceptional typically display extreme highs and lows, spiky testimony of the exceptionalities present for these often struggling individuals.

Other more common disabilities and conditions may be combined with giftedness and may or may not be recognized or diagnosed. These include; dyslexia, dysgraphia, ADD/ADHD (Attention Deficit Disorder, Attention Deficit Hyperactivity Disorder), Asperger's Syndrome, Auditory Processing Disorder, and visual spatial preference, in addition to various physical disabilities (hearing loss, vision problems, ambulatory problems). Misdiagnosis (as learning-disabled, when the "problem" is giftedness) and dual diagnosis (learning-disabled plus giftedness) are not uncommon (Webb, 2005).

UNIQUELY ABLE

The term *creative underachievers* can be used to describe gifted, creative children who do not perform at expected levels, but this may be a misnomer. A better term for this group might be the *creative underserved.* Unconventional but uniquely able learners are capable of unparalleled work, given the right learning environment. The problem, in many cases, does not lie with the child, but with a context of restraint. Teachers often have no knowledge of the profound, unusual interests and talents these individuals harbor, simply because there is no place in school to demonstrate them.

It might be reasonable to assume that art class is an oasis in the regular school day for kids who struggle daily with the challenges, subtleties, and complexities associated with being gifted and creative. In art, creativity is recognized, supported, and developed—right? While it is true that art class may be a welcome haven from the routines of the typical school day, it is also true that in many art classrooms expectations of conformity and compliance are every bit as prevalent as in every other class. The difference in many cases is merely that students get to use paint and clay, not that they have license to make meaningful decisions about their artwork. It is routinely the teacher, not the student, who maintains creative control of the project, manages the materials, works out problems, assigns subject matter, and dictates technique toward a predetermined result. Sometimes there is little left for students to do but carry out the teacher's step-by-step art project, a rather unappealing endeavor for creative children brimming with their own ideas about what to make and how to make it!

Creative kids are, characteristically, extraordinarily self-directed learners. It is difficult for them to sit still and wait for directions and permission to begin. It can be agonizing to follow step-by-step instructions and unbearable to have to wait for the rest of the class to catch up before they can move on. Art students who finish early are routinely confronted with teachers' transparent suggestions to "add more detail" or "try some shading," veiled attempts to stall students who are inconveniently "done" ahead of their classmates. Conversely, some of these learners tend to embark on work that is so complex that the rest of the class is more than ready to move on before these detailed-oriented, big-idea artists are ready to stop. Perfectionist tendencies are common in this population. Students who are perfectionists may need more time to complete their work or even permission to start over, when only this will do. Given what we understand about creative children, and what we know about school norms, it is clear that for them, a typical school setting is not optimal. These students require a fundamentally different approach to learning in a setting that supports their strengths and abilities.

Colangelo, Assouline, and Gross (2004) present an argument for grade-skipping as a simple means to accommodate the academic readiness of gifted students. Likewise, block scheduling may be a good way to accommodate creative students who benefit from greater units of uninterrupted time to incubate ideas and engage in *creative flow* (Csikszentmihalyi, 1996; Hathaway, 2009). But beyond schedules that provide more time, a luxury often out of reach in today's schools, art educators can rethink their teaching methods and restructure their classrooms to better accommodate these unique learners. Programs that feature student choice, flexible use of time, and student-directed learning, and capitalize on emergent curriculum are ideal for gifted, creative students. Programs with these components also benefit students with a myriad of other special needs and all those in between.

CHOICE-BASED ART AND STUDENT-DIRECTED LEARNING

Art used to be a ten—now it's a thousand. (10-year-old boy)

What Is "It"?

What is it that transforms school rebels into ingenious inventors, hooded outliers into expressive painters, confirmed rogues into skilled craftsmen, and kids who hate school into ones who won't let their parents schedule appointments on art day? Knowing and trusting that there is a place in school where their ideas come first and where they can do their important work is radical and compelling for students used to being told to calm down and fit in.

Students in choice-based art programs are encouraged to assume creative control of their art and artmaking processes within an environment designed to support individual inquiry and the development of artistic behavior (Douglas & Jaquith, 2009). Choice-based studio settings offer opportunity for autonomy not often found in regular school programming. It is this feature above all else that empowers bright, creative, but underachieving students to find, develop, and demonstrate hidden strengths and realize personal success. For many, this way of learning within a school setting is unprecedented, causing even the most confirmed rogues to positively gush about their love and gratitude for their choice-based art program (Andrews, 2010; Hathaway, 2009). Choice-based art teachers note that outlaws, rebels, and rogues, in trouble almost everywhere else in school, are engaged and productive learners in art, finally able to shed their armor and set aside their defensive weaponry. Programming featuring individualized, inquiry-based curriculum supports the wide-ranging interests and abilities of this group. Recognizing and supporting strengths, rather than remediating school-exacerbated deficits, results in dynamic, relevant, integrated learning and enthusiastic, eager students.

Students in a learner-directed studio setting work in a manner consistent with practicing artists—they identify ideas and problems of interest; select materials and methods; practice, perfect, and assess their work. In this design, students aren't merely learning *about* art, they are learning *through* art as they assume the role of artists. Students come to understand art and the art world from the inside out as they employ the skills, techniques, and attitudes—the habits of mind, typical of artists (Hetland, Winner, Veenema & Sheridan, 2007). In studio-based classrooms, teachers "place a greater emphasis on balancing authentic content and process, involving students as firsthand inquirers" (Renzulli, Leppien, & Hays, 2000, p. 1). This is a powerful, personal way to learn. In choice-based classrooms, it is the student, not the teacher, who defines the project. Teachers function as facilitators, mentors, co-conspirators, instructors, or cheering squad, depending on the observed need, circumstance, and interests of students. This design comple- ments the original thinking and idiosyncratic approaches typical of creative individuals, and enables disenfranchised students to re-identify as potters, painters, sculptors, and designers.

Autonomy is supported by carefully designed art spaces. Materials, tools, references, and resources are out and available, typically arranged in media-based centers for easy access and management. Personal relevance, choice, and flexible pacing permit students to go deep into their work. These qualities are prescribed by best practice in gifted education (Renzulli et al., 2000; Robinson et al., 2007). Individual learning preferences are honored in a program where everyone is expected to discover and develop their own creative process. The choice-based studio may be the first place in school where passions and outside interests are acknowledged and developed in a meaningful way. The art studio may also be the only place where undirected experimentation and creative play are allowed. Here, creative play is en- dorsed as a legitimate method of inquiry. Discoveries made in this way build knowledge and inform future artwork.

Collaboration and Gifted Students

Last-century models for education championed individual work for in- dividual gain. Contemporary learning standards stress the importance of practicing collaborative work. Collaboration in a choice-based setting is self-selected. This is an important distinction to make when working with gifted children. For these learners, teacher-designated groupings can be problematic and disdained for many reasons, not the least of which is the perception that in teacher-assigned heterogeneous groups, gifted students feel they must carry the group or suffer a poor grade. This causes consider- able stress and resentment. Student-selected pairings in the art studio assure the benefits of collaboration without the negative aspects students dread.

Authentic collaboration in studio classrooms occurs organically when students share interests or simply enjoy working together. Self-selected, col- laborative work can be invigorating and motivating. At times it is clear that the collaboration itself is the important thing, the artwork is secondary to the process of creating it. Students derive immense pleasure from working with like-minded peers on complex projects of mutual delight. For example, a World Cup soccer stadium is planned over summer vacation by two de- voted soccer fans. The passion these two share for the sport is heightened by their first-hand knowledge as athletes. As the work progresses, the project attracts other fans who seek to share what is shaping up to be a big deal.

The newcomers happily toil at the direction of the originators, who now assume a leadership role. The scale-model replica proceeds—complete with corporate sponsors, shopping villages, sculpture installations, and team uniforms—an undertaking that lasts for weeks and engages previously detached students.

In another class, a highly engineered battle scene emerges and captures several unlikely collaborators who usually spend art class in the hall. This group plots and labors for authenticity and impact. They debate possible additions and discuss various aesthetic choices. After 8 weeks, this project grows out of the confines of 1st-period art class. Work now continues in consecutive shifts executed by a revolving crew that meets at recess, during study hall, and after school. These are not typical top-down school art projects detailed in art education journals or illustrated in art teacher handbooks. Instead, these undertakings entail the same kind of real-time planning, implementation, and reflection adult artists use when engaged in authentic artmaking. Projects such as these are personal and important to the groups of students who instigate them and bring them to fruition. Through student-initiated themes and projects, students achieve meaningful curricular goals in an authentic, bottom-up approach.

Specialization, Dwelling, and Mastery

In typical school art programs, students have limited access to the tools and materials—teachers secure these in locked supply closets and dole them out on their own schedule, when the assigned project calls for them. Usually curriculum is designed to be developmental and sequential, and it is the teacher who decides the order of things. The teacher also hands out the appropriate materials and directs their use. Under this construct, students might work with clay once each year to carry out the project their teacher plans. The following year, when clay comes out, another project will be executed to move the student to the next level. In a choice-based class, everyone is introduced to a material or technique, and then students choose which of these to pursue in greater depth. For instance, after clay has been introduced to everyone and the basics established, students who love clay can dwell in the "clay center" for extended, self-determined periods of time. Students who chose to work with the same material, tools, techniques, or themes over an extended period gain knowledge that is only won by perseverance. The result of a learner-differentiated curriculum is that students can go deep into their work and achieve at high levels.

In settings where students self-direct, opportunity exists for genuine specialization and mastery. Furthermore, teachers who are alert to the possibility of emergent curriculum expand learning for individuals and entire classes by framing and extending student-generated themes. Teaching to emergent curriculum creates a vibrant learning community exposed to a great deal more content than is possible when everyone is working on the same project at the same time.

CONCLUSION

The most creative students are also most likely to be at risk in school, where their unusual ability is more hindrance than asset. "A major factor in underachievement is the level of student motivation. Gifted students appear to be more highly motivated in an environment that values learning over pure performance. Schools, however, often value the reverse—performance over learning" (Morando, n.d.). Teacher-directed, whole-group instruction, rigid time schedules, imposed collaboration, extrinsic motivation (reward/punishment), limited student choice, lack of personal relevance, and emphasis on standardized testing are common pedagogical missteps likely to sabotage highly creative students. Art teachers are in a unique position to see the best in these kids and can support them simply by creating a setting for more student-directed learning.

Teachers who understand the importance of student autonomy find unparalleled success with gifted, creative students. Students commonly express both gratitude and relief when they encounter choice-based programming. Finally there *is* a place in school to paint the pictures in their minds; to work at their own pace, in their own way; and to stay with a subject until they are sated. Strong and sometimes secret interests and hobbies from home finally have a valid place in school and a setting in which to flourish. Embers ignited in other disciplines can blaze in art and extend learning toward new, unscripted directions. For the gifted, creative, often misunderstood, and underserved learner, the opportunity to work as an artist in an authentic studio setting can be deeply meaningful and important, sometimes affecting the difference between success and failure in school. This is a powerful way to learn about any subject and may be essential for this group of learners to thrive in school.

Outlaws in the art room, provided with autonomy, choice, space, interesting materials, engaging processes, and time, are empowered to become passionate, intrinsically motivated artists. Notorious school rogues are too engaged in their work to indulge in the shenanigans that earned them their reputations around school. Instead of scheming to confound authoritarian confines or skirt what are perceived as irrelevant tasks, disenfranchised students discover something they are good at, or something they love, or something hard to master but worth the effort. For some, this is transformative. For those at risk or on the brink of dropping out (or being thrown out) of school, choice-based art can literally be the only thing that keeps these students in school. The advantage for this particular population of outlaws, rebels, and rogues (who in reality may really be highly creative, underachieving, misunderstood children) is enormous. The power of student-directed pedagogy demonstrated in the art room is significant and merits consideration across domains, as an elegant way to provide authentically differentiated learning opportunities for all students.

REFERENCES

Andrews, B. H. (2010, July). Student ownership: Learning in a student-centered art room. *Art Education, 63*(4), 40–46.

Betts, G. T., & Kercher, J. K. (1999). *Autonomous learner model: Optimizing ability*. Greeley, CO: Autonomous Learning Publications and Specialists.

Colangelo, N., Assouline, S. G., & Gross, M. U. (2004). *A nation deceived*. Iowa City: The University of Iowa.

Colangelo, N., & Davis, G. A. (2003). *Handbook of gifted education*. Boston: Pearson Education, Inc.

Csikszentmihalyi, M. (1996). *Creativity: Flow and the psychology of discovery and invention*. New York: HarperCollins.

Davis, G. A. (1999). *Creativity is forever*. Dubuque, IA : Kendall/Hunt Publishing Company.

Davis, G. A., & Rimm, S. B. (2004). *Education of the gifted and talented* (5th ed.). Boston: Pearson Education, Inc.

Douglas, K. M., & Jaquith, D. B. (2009). *Engaging learners through artmaking*. New York: Teachers College Press.

Hartmann, T. (2000). Creativity and ADD: A brilliant and flexible mind. In K. Kay (Ed.), *Uniquely gifted: Identifying and meeting the needs of the twice-exceptional student* (pp. 169–172). Gilsom, NH: Avocus Publishing, Inc.

Hathaway, N. E. (2009). Teaching for artistic behavior: Fostering creative possibility. In *Perspectives in gifted education: Creativity* (pp. 68–93). Denver, CO: Institute for the Development of Gifted Education.

Hetland, L., Winner, E., Veenema, S., & Sheridan, K.M. (2007). *Studio thinking: The real benefits of visual arts education*. New York: Teachers College Press.

Morando, K. (n.d.). *Characteristics of underachievement in gifted students*. Available at http://www.northcanton.sparcc.org/~hck/data/dmo1nc/files/num16_Guidance_Underachievement.doc

Renzulli, J. S., Leppien, J. H., & Hays, T. S. (2000). *The multiple menu model: A practical guide for developing differentiated curriculum*. Mansfield Center, CT: Creative Learning Press.

Robinson, K. (2006, February). Ken Robinson says schools kill creativity. *TED Talks* [video]. Available at http://www.ted.com/talks/ken_robinson_says_schools_kill_creativity.html

Robinson, K. (2010, February). Bring on the learning revolution! *TED Talks* [video]. Available at http://blog.ted.com/2010/05/24/bring_on_the_re/

Robinson, A., Shore, B. M., & Enerson, D. L. (2007). *Best practices in gifted education.* Waco, TX: Prufrock Press.

Silverman, L. K. (1993). Techniques for preventive counseling. In L. K. Silverman (Ed.), *Counseling the gifted and talented* (pp. 81–109). Denver, CO: Love Publishing Company.

Torrance, E. P. (2004). The role of creativity in identification of the gifted and talented. In J. Renzulli (Ed.), *Identification of students for gifted and talented programs* (pp. 17–24). Thousand Oaks, CA: Corwin Press.

Twain, M. (2000). In C. Neider (Ed.), *The autobiography of Mark Twain* (p. 181). New York: HarperPerennial Modern Classics.

Webb, J. T. (2005). *Mis-diagnosis and dual diagnosis of gifted children: Gifted and LD, ADHD, OCD, oppositional defiant disorder.* Scottsdale, AZ: Great Potential Press. Available at http://talentdevelop.com/articles/MADDOGC.html

Winebrenner, S. (2000). Special ed or gifted? It may be hard to tell. In K. Kay (Ed.), *Uniquely gifted: Identifying and meeting the needs of the twice-exceptional student* (pp. 68–73). Gilsom, NH: Avocus Publishing, Inc.

CHAPTER 9

Look in the Mirror

Reflecting on Middle School Art

Ilona Szekely

Take a look in the mirror. As a middle school student you are either the ugliest or the prettiest one in the room, depending on momentary changes. One second you feel as if blemishes will overtake your face; the next second you are filled by an urgency for the latest Air Jordans, airlifting you to membership in the popular crowd. Complete with your makeup, accessories, and yes, issues, you are growing and evolving into what every parent and teacher dreads: a teenager. Now step into the art room, where the teacher asks you to explore yourself through an artistic lens.

As the art teacher of middle school students, many things in my repertoire as a seasoned elementary art teacher had to change. Gaining new insight into the importance of self at this level led me to the conclusion that I had to present major concepts in art, illustrated by brief art projects. Due to short durations of time, I could not afford to build expansive art lessons. It was more important to offer students flexibility and the responsibility to work independently as artists. I began to concentrate on providing students opportunities to renew their declining self-confidence as preadolescents by presenting art lessons that were relevant to their lives. The challenge was to find ways to promote independent artmaking and, during the brief periods the students spent in class, to develop lessons that could be further applied to students' pursuits at home. The art room becomes a place to build community, tapping into students' interests and abilities, while deemphasizing more esoteric aesthetic concerns that might hamper motivation.

As a middle school art teacher, I am aware that my art class is potentially my students' last experience with art. Making this a positive and enjoyable class guides all my teaching. There is a chance that a few of my students will elect to take art in high school, but those numbers continue to dwindle. The increasing demand for college preparatory classes and the substitution of arts and humanities for a fine arts requirement, combined with choices between band or sports, make further art studies unlikely for most. In middle school, each lesson and brief sojourn with students has the potential for sparking a lifetime interest in art. The same art class holds the awesome responsibility because missteps could contribute to ending a student's future connections to art by creating a negative experience.

There are developmental factors that can work against art teachers as they try to make a difference and motivate their students to become future artists, museum directors, or art collectors. Universal change occurs around puberty, away from a natural enjoyment and easy identification with artistic behavior to one of inhibition and lack of satisfaction in experiencing and creating art (Gardner, 1994). Adolescence is an extremely sensitive stage, as described by Glenn (1986): "Motivation and driving forces are high at this time, even though self-confidence is lacking" (p. 6). Middle school students may either give up artistic activity altogether, regress significantly, or fully embrace art and immerse themselves in it wholeheartedly. The path a student takes is tied to the result of their middle school art experiences, with the potential to make or break the student's artistic future.

If you walked into my former elementary classroom and asked, "Who is an artist?" practically everyone would enthusiastically cheer and raise a hand. Elementary school students, for the most part, exhibit a high level of creative self-confidence and an insatiable appetite to make art. Typically, there is a support system for elementary school children to be creative at home, backed by an art teacher the students know well, having been the recipients of encouraging remarks for several years. During middle school, academics are clearly defined as the important subjects by signals given by parents and the school. Working with middle school students provides me with a new set of challenges different from those I encountered as an elementary art teacher. This list includes a lack of self-perception as an artist and creative individual, a diminishing interest and time for art, and little support from home or school for the preadolescent artist. These challenges have changed the way I teach at the middle school level and the way I view middle school students.

A MATTER OF TIME

After 6 years at the elementary level, I was accustomed to working with my students for at least a year and up to 6 years if they started with me in kindergarten. I had the time needed to instill in my students a love of art resulting in important artistic independence and self-confidence in their ideas, judgments, and artmaking abilities. It took a while for my students to learn that they should come to art class prepared with materials and ideas and be ready to work on their ideas in a supportive artist-studio. In this environment, we built an artist-to-artist relationship and trust to be able to share street finds, art plans, and ideas. Students realized that their opinions counted and their ideas were listened to and taken seriously in class.

In contrast, the middle school bell shocked my art teaching that had previously depended on extensive time to build special relationships with young artists. For example, I was not used to the middle school pacing of 9-week class rotations. Nor is it easy to adjust to seeing students only once in their school career. Everything is rushed; each moment and every lesson has to be significant. Almost instant relationships and creative trust have to be established, if students are to perform freely and independently in the art room. In a school where students' ideas and opinions are seldom asked for, it is difficult for students to talk freely and share their ideas about anything. There is little time to waste, since developing artistic behaviors and habits, and learning about art and artists, seems overwhelming to condense into a few meetings.

A BIG FISH IN A SMALL POND

In my elementary school, I was a star! As a teacher in charge of a subject everyone loved, I was a celebrity overseeing a program that was not just called *specials*, but was truly considered special by children. Specialty teachers were the core of the school; we did the scheduling and it felt like the school itself revolved around us. Music, physical education, and art were classes students looked forward to all week.

In middle school, my art program is hidden within a large category of electives, even by its designation to be considered a less important subject. I am no longer referred to as a specials teacher; now I am a member of an *Exploratory Team*. By using term *exploratory*, the impression the exploratory teachers receive from the administration is that our subjects are to be explored, but not taken too seriously. Academic areas, called core subjects, clearly designate what matters in the school. Students are divided into teams with special names and symbols that assign team loyalties and are meant to evoke team spirit. Exploratory teachers are not part of these teams, but are a group unto themselves. Students weave through the classes but are never part of the exploratory team. Exploratory teachers work with all grade levels but are not included in either the team spirit or the core of the school. According to research done by Braddock and McPartland (1997), there is an increase in how subject matter is departmentalized, and ability tracking is on the rise in middle school. Our shadow existence reflects our minor role in decision-making and the isolation of art teachers in middle schools.

Considering my new role in middle school, I decided to build community within the school by creating an art club and encouraging students to come to my classroom before and after school. As the only art teacher in school, I realized the need to seek support outside my field. Collaborating with other Exploratory teachers proved to be crucial in building the art program. Involvement in school plays, musical performances, arts days, and events with other teachers and local artists has placed our programs and the importance of these exploratory subjects at the center of our school. Strong collaborations assure stronger art programs.

MEANING AND EXPERIENCE

My elementary students made their own connections between their play, their home creations, their interests, and their home art. The children instinctively had a need and saw reasons for artmaking, finding interesting ways to use their art. In middle school, I have to work hard to make connections between art and my students' interests. Excitement about art and a reason for artmaking cannot be assumed; outreach to students is necessary. Engaging attention and emotions and building enthusiasm about art has to be demonstrated in each lesson. The reasons for making art have to be discussed with students. My middle school students work best in the role of designers, in design teams, and in problem-solving situations. For example, they enjoy the reality of working on presentations for clients. Students especially respond to the role of designers when it involves their personal possessions such as clothing, school supplies, or cell phones. Ideas are easier to elicit in response to student interest than to the discussion of design principles or the old masters. I plan for art projects centered on contemporary teen life, focusing on after-school activities and reaching art interests by students designing equipment for computers and sports, or settings and costumes for fashion shows and rock concerts. Keeping up with students' interests, the latest clothing line, or teen comics in the United States and Japan are important to art class fashion designers and comic book illustrators. References to the mall or involving students' music interests do not impede the required art curriculum. Experiences are created by forming connections to what holds value to students' relevant artmaking. It's simply good middle school teaching practice to use contemporary media and diverse art forms to convey art principles and insure meaningful art discussions.

THE SELF IN ELEMENTARY AND MIDDLE SCHOOL ART

During the middle school years, the self goes through a period of adjustment, leading to a very different kind of art than I was used to in the free-spirited artworks of younger children. My elementary students freely ventured into every form of art, their brushstrokes uninhibited, their lines playful and confident. I was used to this freedom in artmaking and was surprised to find how much preadolescents change in their timid and controlled approaches to art. According to Stokrocki (1997), "The middle school years are times of intense curiosity for preadolescents who are interested in their past, present, and future possibilities" (p. 6). My students appear to be constantly asking themselves questions such as:

Who am I?
What is the image I want portray to the world?
Do I live up to the creative person I want to be?
Who is looking at me?
Who will see my art?

I learn to recognize the usefulness of art during this stage of development to help my students work out their deepest feelings. Crafting art lessons has to take into account students' deep introspection, allowing them to engage in projects that probe themselves within their own comfort level.

My middle school students search for their creative selves by testing their taste and the bounds of personal style. Creative redesigning of their backpacks, nail polish paintings, temporary tattoo designs, or hairstyling innovations are all part of middle school art. These endeavors provide a picture of individuals striving to be creative. I find it important to embrace my students' ability to think creatively in all areas. I make it a point to share students' unique artistic observations and insights, not just in class, but also in what I observe at the mall or on the street. I look to students for inspiration and artistic clues, often finding them in the items they carry to class, or in the decorations they design on their bags or school binders. Students in middle school don't show off their art as freely as my elementary students, who held up and waved their art in front of me. Preadolescents' creative explorations are to be sought.

RELEVANT LESSONS

Now I look more closely and deeply to find the artistic self-expressions of my students. To be effective, states Glenn (1986), "Teachers in middle school have to be sincerely, aggressively active in the instructional process" (p. 7). I watch for personal art forms, individual collections, and design interests that may become incorporated into an art lesson. Based on students' unique displays of buttons and key chains on their school bags, we design our own key chains and art buttons with poetic slogans and expressions. We brainstorm about how to redecorate, reconfigure, or redesign sneakers, shoelaces, and other wearable art forms. I provide a safe haven for adolescents to unload their collections of hidden pocket treasures consisting of handheld electronics, small computer games, cell phone covers, iPods, and Blackberries. Students are adept at considering their electronic companions as potential subjects and tools for contemporary art. As artists and designers, students create imaginative updates of all contemporary gadgets.

Many of my art lessons address fashion choices and design decision-making experiences that promote a search for individual style and artistic independence. My students are keenly aware of current fashion trends in clothes and accessories. These visual skills and awarenesses are turned into artistic opportunities that may be fostered outside of the classroom.

REEXAMINING MIDDLE SCHOOL PORTRAITURE

While my young elementary students loved to make funny, fanciful, and free portraits of themselves and anyone else, this has not been true in middle school. I found early in my middle school teaching that self-portraits provoke preteens' insecurities and doubts, as self-consciousness about appearances is complicated by a desire to draw realistically. Michael (1983) explains:

> When the desire for perceptual reality is accompanied by the psychological changes that occur as a result of the physiological changes brought about by puberty, an awareness comes about on the part of the individual who now consciously and critically looks at his artwork as an adult. (p. 20)

Middle school students are comfortable using technology and media with which they are familiar to create modern self-portraits. In our art class, students employ fax and portable copy machines, e-mail, and Photoshop into their portrait art, and save it all on DVDs. When portraits become entwined with design, technology, and popular culture, the task becomes freeing for preteens. As portrait artists and designers in a contemporary world, preadolescents feel involved and interested to take their place in society. In portraiture and in all of their art, middle school students are futurists and willing commentators on visual culture.

CREATING A POSITIVE AND PRODUCTIVE EXPERIENCE IN SCHOOL AND AT HOME

The middle school art experience can be considered as an extension of elementary art, a preparation for future high school art, and a trial period or an exploratory for the role art will play in students' lives. With proper attention, it is a place where a lifelong love of art can be established. Having worked in a setting where there was the luxury of multiple years to nurture young artists in elementary school, I now face the problem of having to condense the art program into brief middle school rotations. I have just 9 weeks to create lasting impressions, convey the importance of art in students' lives, and confirm their interests and abilities to spend their lives as artistic individuals.

Always in the back of my mind is the importance of using these 9 weeks to improve students' attitudes toward art and their views about themselves as artists. Instead of a focus on specific artmaking techniques or adult art formulas or formal design principles, we discuss broad ideas of what it means to plan, to think, and to live as an artist. My goal for middle school students is for them to see their world through an artistic lens, and to find new ways of responding to their ideas and observations using contemporary media. The challenge lies in assisting middle school students to regain the fun and confidence they had with art when they were younger.

In elementary school students were eager to wrap their art in a fancy package, making it special to take home. Not only does my middle school students' art have to be special, but students need to go home with new art plans and attitudes. Middle school teaching should encourage setting up home art studios, planning home art projects, and building on the experiences touched upon in school. Brief middle school art periods need to inspire artistic thinking and action beyond the school. Students make art projects that can be reinvented at home: projects that can be expanded, used, worn, or displayed in a room. My teaching addresses ways students can prepare for each art class, and how they can extend the art class by using their creative ideas outside of school time. For ideas, students might consider everything from ways to decorate their bedroom to finding a place to display their art in the community.

CONCLUSION

Parting after a 9-week rotation with my students in middle school is never easy. It carries the great responsibility of leaving them prepared to be artists, appreciators, and art collectors on their own. During our final days together we share our art diaries, and design lasting storage cases and books made from student-generated photographs and artworks. Excitement can be created not only about taking artworks home but by preserving the spirit in which they were made, and utilizing that spirit later. When students invest the time to playfully frame some of their art, they share with me where their artworks will hang and how they will be treasured.

In order for students to keep producing art after the 9 weeks are over, it is crucial to instill a sense of artistic independence. My hope is that they might begin to make art on their own, have a renewed confidence in their artistic voice, and form deeper connections to the art world. These students might never have another formal art experience, so if, after our 9 weeks together, their confidence in their abilities is strengthened, the class was a success.

My former elementary students knew they were artists. Middle school art students are firm in the belief that they either are, or definitely not, artists. There may be skepticism in their art, but I also see hope, especially when middle school students are supported, acknowledged, and praised for their work. My middle school students want to be artists, probably as much as my elementary students did, but they seek self-expression in ways that can go unrecognized. Within the safety of conformity, preadolescents look for ways to be themselves. Much of their art, in its intent and beauty, reflects a deeply personal search. Middle school is a time of searching for independence and thus, adolescent art is often hidden or surfaces in untraditional ways.

REFERENCES

Braddock, J. H., & McPartland, J. M.. (1997). Rites of passage for middle school students. *Art Education, 50*(3), 48–55.

Gardner, H. (1994). *The arts and human development: A psychological study of the artistic process.* New York: Basic Books.

Glenn, D. (1986). The middle school: Art, the transient child and the role of the teacher. *Art Education, 39*(5), 4–7.

Michael, J. (1983). *Art and adolescence: Teaching art at the secondary level.* New York: Teachers College Press.

Stokrocki, M. (1997). Rites of passage for middle school students. *Art Education 50*(3), 48–55.

CHAPTER 10

Teaching for Innovation

Supporting Diverse
Learning Communities

Ellyn Gaspardi

Traditionally students in public school art classrooms are given an art assignment that all must complete. The teacher designs the lesson, gathers the
supplies, gives motivational demonstrations and examples, and then coach-
es students to be able to make the preconceived end product. Any students
who face physical or mental challenges are given an adapted version of the
project, and they do the best that they can. This type of instruction trains
students to follow directions to produce a specific product. These skills,
highly valued during the 20th century, no longer address the needs of a 21st-
century workforce. In addition, the whole-group approach does not connect
with increasingly diverse student bodies.

In contrast, choice-based studio classrooms allow for success on many
levels for all learners, embedding Universal Design for Learning concepts
while encouraging practice in 21st-century skills. How do choice-based
teachers meet diverse needs while offering students opportunities to do the
real work of artists? For answers, we can look to the art room at the Wil-
liams Intermediate School. Here, four classes of middle school students attend art for an hour each day, for 12-week trimesters. This chapter examines
one of these groups, consisting of 37 students. These students come to art
class with two adult paraprofessionals who normally work one-on-one with
a particular student. Nine students in this class are on extensive Individual
Education Plans. There are additional students with learning differences,
including one student with Down syndrome, one student with autism, one
student with Asperger's syndrome, two English language learners, and four
other students facing complex personal challenges. The remaining students
have various other issues that they deal with on a daily basis, not to men-

tion the difficulty of just finding a seat in such a large class! Despite many challenges, these students function very well in this learner-directed classroom. They are able to work independently and are meeting the curriculum criteria.

At the beginning of each class the teacher presents information and updates, after which students explore newly introduced art materials or choose independent work. Students get right up and find their unfinished work from previous classes, or gather materials and resources for new projects. They work in groups or alone. Some engage in conversation about their art while others work quietly in their own space. This structure allows the teacher to circulate and work with small groups. One group of boys works on a group skateboard project; others have finished their version of a hockey board game and they are testing it out. A few girls are painting a mural together. The variety of projects and working styles reflects the diverse interests and abilities of this group.

The structure of the studio classroom is in place from the first day. Students receive focused information and demonstrations that support idea formation, time management, and setup and cleanup procedures, as well as new techniques and materials. The consistent arrangement of space, availability of materials, and structure of both whole-group instruction and studio time sustain student autonomy within this classroom setting.

CHOICE-BASED ART TEACHING SUPPORTS UNIVERSAL DESIGN FOR LEARNING

Although this classroom seems naturally to run smoothly, there is a subtle and complex structure underlying the success students enjoy. Choice-based classrooms are each unique, reflecting the students, the individual teacher, and the school setting. In order to meet the artistic and learning needs of a diverse study body, choice-based teachers use principles very much like those of Universal Design for Learning (UDL). The National Center on Universal Design for Learning defines UDL as: "a scientifically valid framework for guiding educational practice that provides flexibility in the ways information is presented and reduces barriers in instruction while maintaining high expectations for all students" (National Center on Universal Design for Learning [UDL], 2009). Choice-based teachers present information in multiple forms, encourage students to show what they know in diverse ways, and, most importantly, connect with and celebrate student interests. This leads to engagement through intrinsic motivation. The UDL guidelines of reproduction, expression, and engagement (UDL, 2009) enable teachers to support successful outcomes for diverse learners. These strategies exemplify good teaching practices for all students.

CHOICE-BASED TEACHING SUPPORTS
DIFFERENTIATED LEARNING

When David first started coming to art he would only draw the Pokémon characters that had become his obsession. David's experience is not unusual; stories like his are repeated in choice-based classrooms year after year. David is a student with autism. Uncomfortable in crowds, he has difficulty retrieving words to communicate verbally with others. He exhibits self-stimming behaviors and occasionally when life is overwhelming, David has a meltdown. With gentle encouragement, David branched out into making collages of his favorite Pokemon characters. After some time in the art room David began to relax. He stopped self-stimming behaviors and started to arrive excited and full of ideas. He especially loved recycled sculpture and the hot glue gun. He began to demonstrate flexibility in his thinking as he searched through materials and considered the possibilities. David's ideas were so playful and unique that other students took notice. David began to interact with them and they began to invite him to collaborate on projects. At the end of the trimester David not only participated in a group project, but he volunteered to be the spokesperson for the group. David's teacher in the Life Skills/Connections classroom observes:

> In the choice art room my students are able to work off of their strengths. All of the students see each other's ideas and my students have gone from saying "I can't" to "I can." The regular education students don't see my students as different anymore. They say "Hi" to them in the hallway and comment "Nice boat you made in art today, David." It's their time to shine. (J. Bianchini, personal communication, February 23, 2010)

At the request of his teachers and parents, David will remain in the choice art room for the rest of the year, instead of just one trimester, due to all the growth that occurred for him in this affirming atmosphere.

In student-directed learning, children become problem finders. Choice-based art programs create an environment to encourage students' questions. It becomes the teacher's job to help students translate those questions into insight and understanding (Speicher, 2009). Choice-based environments also engage students in material that has personal relevance. Because students all start at different places and learn at different rates, it is necessary to differentiate without compromising the quality of the learning environment. In classes where all voices, ideas, and problems are heard equally, but answered differently, equality does not mean sameness (Speicher, 2009). A choice-based structure helps to build a learning community where students of all abilities feel honored and vital to what is happening in their world.

CHOICE-BASED ART TEACHING SUPPORTS 21ST-CENTURY SKILLS

As technology alters the global landscape, societal and student needs are constantly changing. It is imperative that teachers stay informed about the skills students will need when they leave the classroom. The Partnership for 21st Century Skills was created to address this issue by outlining target skills and providing resources for teachers so they may implement 21st-century skill practice (Partnership for 21st Century Skills, 2004). By looking closely within a typical choice-based art room, evidence of this practice can readily be seen (Teaching for Artistic Behavior, 2009). Each of the following anecdotes demonstrates how choice-based pedagogy supports "21st Century Student Outcomes" as identified by the Partnership for 21st Century Skills (2004).

Creativity and Innovation

A group of girls came to the art classroom with a drawn plan for a sculpture that they wanted to make in art class. This type of inventing and testing of hypotheses happens on a daily basis in a student-directed classroom. Some of these plans succeed, coming out just the way students envisioned. Others are a success because of mistakes and failures that motivate the students to self-correct and rework. Alyssa and Katelyn designed a marble run that looked great on paper but needed lots of adjustment when they tried it in three-dimensional form. It was an opportunity for them to create and then recreate until they were satisfied.

Critical Thinking and Problem-Solving

Ben worked long and hard on models of swimming pools. He was particularly interested in using real water and seeing if he could get it to move from source to pool. This problem-solving activity and the way the artist explained his process was useful as a means to reinforce his critical thinking skills. Ben found the art class to be a place where he continued to feel "smart" even as he struggled in his other classes.

Communication and Collaboration

In the 21st-century working world it is important to be able to function productively in groups, hear other ideas, consider other options, and discover strengths and weaknesses of colleagues. In the art room, teacher and students continually discuss strategies for navigating the world of collaboration and communication. Students choose their own groups and are free to work with those who share their interests. Sometimes middle schoolers discover that their friends aren't the best partners for the job. David was recruited to work with a group of students with whom he rarely engaged outside of class. Because of his previously demonstrated strengths in painting and building, David was asked to join in this project, which, in turn, opened the doorway to new friendships.

Flexibility and Adaptability

Students really hone their ability to change direction and be open to alternate solutions in the course of artmaking in a choice-based studio classroom. This is more important than ever; with many schools focused on test preparation, divergent thinking has taken a back seat. Without practice, students find it harder and harder to look into the many information files within their brains to put together unique solutions (Bartel, 2007). They become less self-reliant and unsure of their own powers to solve a problem. In a choice-based setting, the steps and solutions for artmaking problems are handled by students as they look for individual solutions to their unique creative challenges.

Initiative and Self-Direction

Bruce is a student with Down syndrome. Most of his day he is shadowed by a paraprofessional, but in art class, she usually steps aside. Bruce is very adept at getting his own materials and choosing what he would like to do in art each day. In fact, Bruce knows that art can make him feel better. Sometimes if he is having a difficult day he will come into art and just paint and hum. He is not focused on product on those days—he just enjoys the meditative action of painting. When he is humming his teachers know he is happy. Over time Bruce has initiated a variety of projects including drawing with rulers and templates, painting, and later, cutting up and collaging pieces of his paintings. He has recruited other students to help him complete a sculpture of a city. Art class is the only place in school where Bruce exerts full control over the way he spends his time and, as a result, his work reflects his interests and abilities.

Social and Cross-Cultural Skills

Children who rarely interact with each other outside the studio will sometimes join forces for a particular project. When students work with a new group of partners, they expand their scope and gain new perspectives and new skills. The nature of the choice classroom helps to break down barriers by eliminating competition and the added stress of completing a project that resembles everyone else's solutions. Students are encouraged to share, collaborate, and coach each other. They see first-hand a variety of answers to the same question. Students learn that recognizing one's own weaknesses can be a strength, and that sharing and searching for solutions with others benefits all.

Productivity and Accountability

In the beginning of the trimester, students understand what is expected of them. It is the student's job to create the work and maintain a portfolio that can be reviewed with their teacher. Some students prefer to have a checklist as a way to keep track of their work, while others might need frequent portfolio checks in order to keep track of their progress. It is expected that students will spend time talking about and analyzing their work. This is done alone and as a group. Students ask questions, give comments, and defend their decisions. When students take the germ of an idea, bring it to reality, and then present their work to the group, they gain confidence in themselves and also learn to be open to the ideas of others.

Leadership and Responsibility

Ben had been a sit-in-the-back-of-the-room kind of kid who had struggled academically for most of his life. One of his art ideas moved him from the back to the front of the room as a leader whose expertise was highly sought after by other students. Ben came to art one day and announced that he had heard a moose call while visiting Maine and he wanted to make a something to imitate that sound. He gathered a can and a string and then recruited Bruce to help him drill a hole in the can and tie in the string. Pulling on the string produced a faint noise, and through experimentation Ben decided to get the string wet. This was the trick! The moose sound bellowed from the can and soon everyone wanted a moose call. Ben taught the class and then went on to experiment with different containers and different strings to get a variety of noises. After that day, Ben was included in a lot of projects, and had no problem moving about the art room and coming up with ideas. The day that he needed a reminder to settle down made his teacher secretly smile. Through increased confidence, Ben had changed his status in the classroom and his view of himself in the group.

Research and Inquiry

Ideas take time. Demystifying the path to innovation is something the choice-based teacher must take on in order for students to believe that they have the power to create ideas and solve problems that may arise during that creation. Teachers need to frequently revisit the many ways that people come up with ideas. Many artists look at other artists' work or research images of a particular subject. Sometimes the materials themselves spark an idea. In some classrooms students play games that generate information about their own lives that can then be used in their work. In the 21st-century work world collaboration, creative exploration and play are methods that successful design companies use to keep ideas flowing and to solve problems (Brown, 2009).

ASSESSMENT

In a choice-based classroom there are a variety of ways to address assessment, depending on the age group and requirements of a particular school. Because this environment is naturally collaborative, it is important that teamwork continues in the assessment process. In addition to traditional rubrics, choice-based teachers often document through photographs, journals, note-taking, examples of student work, and one-on-one conferencing. Digital and physical portfolios are additional ways to view progress over time.

Student-directed learning produces a variety of projects. When students come up with the idea it is imperative that they be given an opportunity to self-assess. This could be in the form of a simple list of questions to ask themselves or an interview. In a noncompetitive atmosphere, students will feel comfortable answering honestly, and then teacher and student can decide on the next course of action. With the variety of approaches established through implementation of Universal Design for Learning strategies, the opportunity for 21st-century skill-building is embedded in every art class.

CONCLUSION

In order to think creatively and divergently students must have time and space to practice 21st-century skills. Discovering new and unique ideas becomes harder if these skills are not utilized. This ability can also be hampered by an atmosphere that cultivates fear and judgment. It is within fear and judgment that conforming and playing it safe become the preferred choices. Many teachers today must rate students on efficiency, memorization, ability to follow directions without questioning, and test scores. This pedagogy creates a setting with few options for exhibiting personal strengths, and fewer opportunities for innovation. If students do not find success within these narrow confines, they disengage from their learning and are sometimes just "not there" literally and figuratively.

Choice-based studio classrooms are accepting, flexible environments where Universal Design for Learning principles guide teachers. In these learning environments, middle school students can fully engage in their work through intrinsic interests. Children like David or Ben learn to embrace mistakes as a way to find answers. They welcome diverse solutions to a problem, and practice a fluidity of thinking that lays the foundation for innovative thought. Students come to class ready and willing to learn because they feel safe, valued, and capable (Douglas & Hathaway, 2007). The self-directed classroom becomes a veritable think tank where all students' skills and knowledge have a place to synthesize into workable real-life solutions and new ideas. Students feel ready to push the limitations of materials and thought processes to which they have been exposed. This is when and where the sparks of innovation ignite. As teachers it is our responsibility to fan this spark through our teaching practices and our daily interactions with our students.

REFERENCES

Bartel, M. (2007). *The secrets of generating art ideas: An inside out art curriculum.* Available at http://www.bartelart.com/arted/ideas.html

Brown, T. (2009). *Change by design: How design thinking transforms organizations and inspires innovation.* New York: HarperCollins.

Douglas, K. M., & Hathaway, N. (2007, March). *Think about it: How school rebels and others find success in the choice-based art class.* Session presented at the 47th annual convention of the National Art Education Association, New York.

National Center on Universal Design for Learning. (2009). *UDL Guidelines, Version 1.0.* Available at http://www.udlcenter.org/aboutudl/udlguidelines/introduction#intro_learners

Partnership for 21st Century Skills. (2004). *Framework for 21st century learning.* Available at http://www.21stcenturyskills.org/index.php

Speicher, S. (2009). *IDEO's 10 tips for creating a 21st century classroom experience.* Available at http://www.metropolismag.com/story/20090218/ideos-ten-tips-for-creating-a-21st-century-classroom-experience

Teaching for Artistic Behavior. (2009). *Teaching for artistic behavior supports 21st century skills.* Available at http://teachingforartisticbehavior.org/21stcenturyskills.html

CHAPTER 11

The Secret Art of Boys

Clyde Gaw

"Bomb!" 7-year-old John warns his classmates. "Kaboom!" He fires pretend magic marker missiles into hostile army figures depicted on a large piece of paper. John rearms himself with oil pastels and unloads a burst of machine gun bullet lines into the battle zone. "Tffffffff, tffffffff!" He loads a stubby brush with tempera paint and thrusts it into blast fragments of jagged lines and shapes. "Look at that! A bomb! He got shot!" One of the characters in the battle scene is wounded. "Kaboom!" John's collaborators, Frank and Jimmy, enter the fray. The trio of make-believe warriors rearm themselves with new magic markers and slice colorful lines into the picture. During an exchange of simulated gun and missile fire, the energetic war artists decide to expand their drawing with more paper and glue. While the battle rages into new territory, more soldiers, tanks, and fighter jets are added. The boys' effort to depict their imaginary conflict intensifies. Soon the enlarged drawing resembles a Cy Twombly[1] abstraction. Classmates are invited over to view the drawing and the boys excitedly share stories about their picture. After two more class sessions, the battle illustrators use crayon-resistant painting techniques, adding colored pencil and more oil pastel. Paper towels are used to blend areas representing fire and smoke. The boys are physically and emotionally in the imaginary battle, immersing themselves in the roles of U.S. military personnel with weapons of power. The boys' teacher transcribes their stories into artist statements:

> *John*: It started with a little battle with Frank and Jimmy. And then we started to connect a big thing. I started the very, very first one and then we connected it.
>
> *Frank*: This is a tank and somebody drew over it, but I could draw over it again because there was a replacement tank. I air-striked their ship.
>
> *Jimmy*: In this one part, there is a flying tank, and he shot the bad

guys' ship. The bad guys had 100 ships, 50 on each side. So we shot both the wings off so they would all be dead.

At the county art show, the boys proudly show their collaborative 20-square-foot multimedia drawing to family members. They soon discover that theirs is the largest two-dimensional work, and among the most visually exciting in the entire 5,000-piece, K–12 art exhibit. Proud parents take pictures of their sons next to the huge drawing, followed by comments of approval and congratulations on a job well done. Back in the classroom after the exhibit, the boys negotiate to divvy up the mural; they cut it into pieces and take their favorite parts home.

FANTASY AND PLAY

Boys are socially conditioned and biologically hardwired to weave action, drama, and danger into their imaginary realms. All children have unique differences of mind (Gardner, 1983; Kandel, 2006; Pinker, 2002). Although girls, too, are attracted to fantasy violence, it is more often the boys who bedevil teachers, parents, and school administrators with their passion for violent content in the games they play, literature they read, and art they create. Under the guidance of educators who facilitate personalized pathways to creative experience (Brooks & Brooks, 1999; Douglas & Jaquith, 2009; Hathaway, 2008), boys will thrive in learning environments where ideas related to superheroes, monsters, villains, military action, and other aspects of their make believe worlds can be expressed.

Just as fantasy violence can be a part of children's play, including cops and robbers, superheroes, or war play (Brown & Vaughn, 2009; Gurian & Stevens, 2005; Jones, 2002; Kindlon & Thompson, 2000), children will express fantasy violence in the art they create (Duncum, 1989; Lowenfeld & Britain, 1971; Rubin, 2005). Many educators, who might consider such content inappropriate for school and resort to censorship, miss out on opportunities to integrate and synthesize essential learning. Art teachers sensitive to child-centered learning may view children's decisions to express fantasy violence as a normal part of their behavior, and may view such events as a means to facilitate deep educational and creative growth experiences.

CHOICE-BASED ART EDUCATION:
A STRUCTURE TO EXPRESS THE INEXPRESSIBLE

One of the profound aspects of choice-based art education pedagogy is authorizing children to create art within an environment dedicated to student-centered learning (Douglas & Jaquith, 2009). The choice-based art education approach facilitates the transmission and construction of knowledge from multiple sources and provides a structure for children to think and operate independently. Students are able to conduct their learning activities in environments that encourage self-direction. In this setting, children know their ideas are important and that their teacher is in their corner (Douglas & Hathaway, 2007). Students are introduced to the concept that artists generate ideas from observation, experimentation, feelings and emotions, memories, and imagination. These sources of creative inspiration provide a framework for children to experience art education on a personally relevant level. Choice-based teachers respect students' individuality, and provide an atmosphere of trust and caring where children share deep thoughts and ideas through their art. In this context, art about weaponry, battles, and fighting can be explored in safety under the watchful guidance of a supportive teacher.

A RATIONALE FOR CHOICE

Traditional teacher-directed approaches to art education assume children are all equally motivated to participate in linear sequences of learning activities. While this approach provides teachers with a convenient structure to plan and deliver curriculum, contingencies for building knowledge upon diverse individual student interests and strengths are often neglected. Many students find didactic art education learning experiences unsatisfying. Behaviorist control mechanisms are typically employed in order to make students comply with contrived teacher directives. Mike, a 5th-grade boy, comments on his previous art education experience: "When I was at my other school, being creative was especially frowned upon. I made an alien clown and I got a D! One time we were making self-portraits, and the teacher said 'If you don't do it right, you will have to do another one.' I used red and she said 'Don't use red. You did it the wrong way.' It just makes me feel mad. My art wasn't appreciated there."

Traditionalists defend teacher-directed approaches because curriculum and instruction can be efficiently delivered and artistic products appear to be of high quality; however, students at a fundamental level are not in control. In fact, students are left outside the decision-making processes central to the very ideas they express. Considerations for balancing structure while developing a least restrictive environment are essential in order to fully engage children's creative experiences.

Within any general education classroom there are opportunities to optimize learning experiences based on students' unique strengths and interests. Teachers who implement static adult-directed learning activities may not consider that children are emotionally connected and highly motivated to work on a multitude of personally relevant self-directed activities. Many such learning activities are related to the integration of science, technology, engineering, and math (STEM), as well as language arts content. For example, in a choice-based environment, one class of 5th-graders might be engaged in multiple learning activities simultaneously. Eight boys in the class are producing scale-model catapults based on their knowledge of Leonardo da Vinci's famous invention drawings. Four girls are building a large cardboard dollhouse complete with furnishings and accessories. Two girls have a passion for writing and editing a monthly newsmagazine. Six boys and three girls are planning and creating scale-model cities and other architectural structures out of wooden blocks. A group of students are producing detailed drawings of animals and insects from illustrated zoology books, while yet another group of boys is interested in creating graphic novels about mythical heroes, monsters, and aliens engaged in conflict.

Choice-based pedagogy aligns with 21st-century learning practices and these learning environments can be thought of as *umwelts* (Cunningham, 1992), places where children are emotionally connected, secure, and willing to share unsolicited personal thoughts and ideas through their art. Choice-based art teachers will observe those individuals who, in traditional settings, might be unmotivated, disengaged, or reluctant learners, thrive in authentic studio settings where they are able to fuse new learning to personal ideas related to their fantasy worlds (Gaw & Douglas, 2010).

Choice-based art teachers value children's idiosyncratic thought, and are responsive to the cognitive diversity in the heterogeneous populations they serve. Inspirational and life-altering student-directed learning experiences, relevant to the child, can be lost forever if opportunities to develop time-sensitive ideas are not supported. Nothing in education is more powerful than authentic student-directed learning experiences constructed from the bottom up.

FANTASY VIOLENCE

Since 2004, children's self-directed art activities have been closely monitored at New Palestine Elementary School in central Indiana. Subject matter varies and includes conflict, battles, war, fighting, monsters, aliens, and other themes related to fantasy violence. Electronic portfolios are used to document, examine, and assess student art activities (Fralick & Gaw, 2008). Substantial evidence in the form of reflective writing, photography, video, audio recordings, and other anecdotes supports the claim that creatively and developmentally, learners thrive in choice-based art programs. Children are observed by parents and teachers to be highly motivated during the design and implementation process of their own learning activities. Inspired children often take their self-directed experiences from art class and continue them as unsolicited activities at home. Conversely, students are able to build upon their home art experiences in the choice art room (Szekely, 2006).

For many boys fantasy violence is a natural part of the repertoire for self-expression. Teachers engage students with questions about the nature of the fantasy art they express. When reflective thinking is stimulated, story narratives and ideas can be explained and the intent of the artists can be examined. Six-year-old Joe has been creating a series of drawings based on his observations and knowledge of penguins. He discusses the story narrative with his art teacher:

Joe: This is the water, see this up here? That's the ice cave where the penguin lives. He fell out of the ice cave, and then to the water. See this purple stuff? That's the stingray's power to make. . . .
Teacher: Stingray?!
Joe: Yeah, that is a stingray, and the stingray, when he gets his power, he can sting the penguin. This yellow stuff will keep the penguin alive, but there is too much purple stuff, so the penguin might die and he might live.
Teacher: What would happen if the stingray went away?
Joe: If the stingray went away, then the penguin would live, but if he would sting the penguin, then he would go ahhhhh. . . .
Teacher: Oh my gosh!
Joe: He would float down into the bottom of the ocean and die.
Teacher: That is such a sad story. Why is the story so sad?
Joe: The story is sad because the stingray might kill the penguin, and penguins are real cute.

In an atmosphere of trust and support, boys will respond positively by producing profound works of art inspired from deep within their psychoemotional realms. Essential knowledge, skills, and educational content can be woven into these personally meaningful learning episodes. There is much educational gold to mine from children's fantasy worlds.

PRETEND WEAPONS PLAY

Many adults have a limited comfort zone to tolerate boys' authentic art related to pretend weapons play. However, boys have legitimate needs to express ideas related to imaginary weapons. The United States is one of the most violent countries in the world. Boys are socialized in our society to protect their families and their country. Looming in boys' minds is the prospect of a showdown with bad guys or prospective enemies. Boys are able to relieve some of their anxiety through their art. Seven-year-old Jimmy shares his cardboard sculpture creation with his art teacher:

Jimmy: Look! This is my sword and shield!
Teacher: What is it for?
Jimmy: This is what I use to battle the monsters.
Teacher: Where do the monsters live?
Jimmy: In my bedroom closet.

Boys have an innate awareness to prepare for future confrontations and are painfully aware of their physical shortcomings. Hindered by underdeveloped adolescent and preadolescent bodies, boys need pretend objects of power in order to level the playing field (Jones, 2002).

Boys' fascination with imaginary weapons can be observed in their fantasy art. Nine-year-old Chuck, a diminutive boy new to the school district, discusses the story narrative behind his pencil drawing:

Teacher: What's happening here?
Chuck: Well, if you must know, the Americans are attacking the
    Japanese outpost here, while the Americans have a little base of
    their own here to the far right.
Teacher: Where's that base, over here in this area?
Chuck: I'm still working on that sniper, 'cause as you can see, his head
    is kind of missing.
Teacher: Oh my.
Chuck: Yeah. Here. Just let me draw his head. (Chuck draws the
    figure's head.)
Teacher: Oh yes. There he is. That's a fancy weapon that he's got.
    What kind of weapon is that?
Chuck: Sniper rifle.
Teacher: Mmm. Okay.
Chuck: It's got six bullets per clip.
Teacher: Oh. Wow. That looks like a lot of action going on in this one.
    Look at this firefight.
Chuck: That right there is an armored personnel carrier—APC for
    short.
Teacher: How do you know all the military language?
Chuck: I just play a lot of war games.
Teacher: Well, I can't wait to see your drawing after it is completed.
Chuck: Sometimes I improvise and make weapons of my own.

Chuck had revealed to his art teacher that he played video games related to the U.S. military and knew a great deal about military history. In addition to the pencil drawings, Chuck created computer drawings of imaginary battles and had some of the most complex story narratives to tell about them. As one of the new students in school, he began the year as an outsider. He tried very hard to make personal connections with his new classmates, but sometimes tattled on the boys he most wanted to befriend. Chuck's unfolding talent for improvisation and storytelling was soon realized and came to fruition near the end of the year when he captivated everybody with a series of film vignettes. Chuck was successful in reconnecting with the boys whom he had tattled on earlier and recruited them to participate in a series of crime drama movies he would star in and direct. The boys proudly showed their films to classmates, who enjoyed the intense acting and action-packed scenes. When the filming was over Chuck and James discussed new ways to improve their next film:

> *James*: Look, once we all die, we come back to harvest his soul.
> *Chuck*: No, James. No demons in the movie.
> *James*: What's wrong with the grim reaper?
> *Chuck*: No, we aren't doing that.
> *James*: Chuck? If you move him (points to the wooden hostage sculpture) to right here (points to a wooden block tower built by another classmate), so that the blocks don't fall over and break that, you know? And then it breaks and falls on that and then that breaks that.
> *Chuck*: Well, it's okay. It's okay.

Earlier in the school year James had ignored Chuck, but was now one of Chuck's main collaborators in the movie productions. Chuck's humorous crime drama films were viewed by the class with much enjoyment. Chuck, who had begun the year as an anxious outsider, was now accepted by his classmates as very special and unique.

FINDING OUT WHAT I'M GOOD AT

In choice-based art programs, where sculpture opportunities abound, it is not uncommon for boys to invent simple machines or create sculptures with moving parts at the construction centers. David, a 5th-grade student also new to school, took advantage of the construction center materials soon after discovering his talent for designing and assembling three-dimensional cardboard and plastic sculptures. While watching other students experiment with catapult construction, David began to envision his own catapults and assembled them with notches, slots, and hot glue. He expanded his art activities to his home studio after convincing his father to buy him a hot glue gun. These experiences led to other projects including a large, detail-oriented cardboard castle, complete with a 24-inch cylinder-shaped tower. Despite his difficulty in other subject areas, David later informed his art teacher that he knew he was good at working with his hands.

Choice-based art programs allow children to discover and work from their strengths. Creating authentic works of art requires conceptualization skills and capability to execute and represent ideas in two, three, or four dimensions. Developing the capacity to envision and focus attention on a vast array of details is a major intellectual achievement.

SAFELY EXPRESSING ONE'S FEELINGS

Because most of the school day is devoted to academic pursuits transmitted through didactic learning and assessments, a premium is placed on children to stay quiet, sit still in their seats, and listen to the teacher. Children rarely have an opportunity to express themselves in such a closed atmosphere that values compliance over self-direction. The choice-based art room is that special place in the school where children have license to investigate self-generated ideas related to their artistic pursuits. This can be a safe place for boys to explore themes related to conflict and fantasy violence. One of the important outcomes of self-directed artmaking is active thinking. Children are actively conceiving new ideas and uses for materials, and can articulate detailed verbal or written responses of their experiences. Children have compelling stories to share about their fantasy art when given opportunities to conceive them in supportive environments that stimulate a child's sense of belonging and connectedness.

CRACKING DOWN ON BOYS

Children may secretly hide their fantasy art or deny its existence at school because they know their art ideas are considered taboo. Zero tolerance policies abound in schools across the United States today. Boys learn to lie about their secret art or develop feelings of confusion, anxiety, and insecurity. In many educational institutions, adults are fearful of boys. Some adults believe children who express ideas related to mass media or video game violence might turn into perpetrators of violence. They consider young males as prospective troublemakers who might not know the difference between fantasy and reality. Boys can be censored, reprimanded, and even suspended by authorities who view their school art containing fantasy violence as inappropriate. In 2007, a 13-year-old Arizona boy received a 5-day suspension for making an innocuous doodle drawing of a gun on the margins of his assignment paper in science class (*World Net Daily*, August 22, 2007). The drawing contained no observable written threats or text. School officials claimed the boy's drawing was "considered a threat." The boy's parents argued to administrators that more harm than good was being done by the punishment. Acts of suppression and negative reinforcement can exacerbate feelings of frustration, anxiety, and aggression. Adults in schools run the risk of losing the credibility of their boys when they subject them to misguided punitive actions (Gurian & Stevens, 2005; Kindlon & Thompson, 2000).

VIDEO GAME CONTROVERSY

A brief discussion of video games and their influence on boys is pertinent to this discourse. Many boys are game players and are inspired to create art from their gaming experiences. Concerns that video game and media violence desensitize and influence children to commit violent action are widespread. There have been many attempts to link video games to lethal violence by researchers, politicians, concerned citizens, and news media. *NBC Nightly News* reported that Chicago street violence is so bad, two state lawmakers recommend calling out the National Guard to patrol inner-city Chicago neighborhoods in order to keep the peace (NBC, April 26, 2010). Directly after the Chicago street violence report on the same broadcast, NBC News introduced a new story on video game fantasy violence and suggested video game players are responsible for increased violence across the country. Most criminologists, psychologists, and sociologists who have studied this problem know better.

It is important to remember there are tens of millions of game players in the United States of all ages who do not commit acts of violence and are non-aggressive, law-abiding citizens and contributing members of society. How do video game detractors account for the violence and criminal activity enacted throughout human history long before video games and mass media were invented? Just as comic books and progressive education were once blamed for increased juvenile delinquency in the 1940s and 1950s, video games are now in the crosshairs of those interested in an easy fix to a complex social problem. If the theory that mass media and video games unduly influence children to commit acts of violence has substantial merit, then incidents of school and community violence would be exponentially greater than current rates. According to the U.S. Bureau of Justice and the

FBI, rates of juvenile violent crime have decreased since the late 1990s, a period of significant video game playing expansion (Office of Juvenile Justice and Delinquency Prevention, 2008).

While video games remain an easy target to blame for the epidemic of violence in the United States, the root causes are connected to wicked social problems and are more difficult to address. Children who are subjected to inhumane living conditions or suffer from mental illness, real violence, cruelty, and bullying are at major risk for engaging in violent behavior (Hollowell, 2008; Kindlon & Thompson, 2000).

SAFETY CONSIDERATIONS

When rare events of lethal violence are fully examined, the motivations for committing such heinous acts are clearly related to revenge motives and victim mentalities. A common thread in these acts is the transmission of actual threats in spoken or written forms. Other red flags to consider in the context of an individual's normal behavior might include changes in their appearance and changes in friends, frequent use of inappropriate language, changes in personal habits, changes in humanitarian or religious values, and episodes where individuals are quick to anger, cry, or reveal other unstable emotions (Hollowell, 2008). Maintaining a safe learning environment is the responsibility of all educators, as the vast majority of children are deserving of adults' trust. It is very important for children to have the opportunity to make their own choices at school in order to facilitate ownership of their learning experiences. Encouraging students to share their ideas and stories when they create art with fantasy violence allows adults to see just what they are doing with those fantasies. When children make verbal or written threats toward others and combinations of personality and behavioral changes are observed, action is warranted. In the event a child makes reference to other individuals with statements of intent to do real harm, those threats need to be taken seriously. Communicating with parents, social workers, administrators, and, ultimately, law enforcement is paramount in order to prevent potential acts of real violence.

PATHWAYS TO CREATIVE EXPERIENCE

Fantasy violence and play violence are simply fantasy and play. Play is a natural form of learning and one of the ways children learn best. Play is fundamental to intellectual development. It is not uncommon for children to play with art ideas, materials, and techniques in choice-based art rooms.

The concern that real violence can be triggered in children who engage in artistic activity contradicts what we know about creativity. Paradoxically, creativity can be nurtured and developed through self-directed activities related to fantasy violence to stimulate forms of active thinking. When immersed in streams of consciousness where fantasy violence is part and parcel of an artistic endeavor, a child's psychological state is more attuned to heightened states of play than to states of criminal deviance. The creative process strengthens children's self-confidence as new concepts, objects, ideas, and performance skills are born from individual or collaborative efforts. Conceiving and solving artistic problems in a state of creative flow has the effect of releasing tensions and anxiety, and ameliorating violent or aggressive dispositions (Csikzentmilhalyi, 1996; Lowenfeld & Britain, 1971; May, 1975; Rubin, 2005). From this standpoint, teachers should not be afraid to provide children with as much latitude as possible for expressing personally relevant art ideas, including those with fantasy violence. Acceptance or rejection of student's ideas about fantasy violence is not a black-and-white issue. Getting to know children by the content and range of their art is a distinctive characteristic of choice-based art education pedagogy and provides teachers with first-hand knowledge of their students' intellectual, creative, and behavioral capacities.

CONCLUSION

The psychological foundations of meaningful learning are based on emotional connections. Coercing students to comply with educational activities in which they have no input, and rendering them as passive recipients of knowledge, is problematic. Not only does it limit what students are capable of creating and learning, it removes them from the experience of designing and solving their own artistic problems. One cannot make the claim that art education experiences empower students to become independent thinkers if they are left out of the decision-making processes central to the ideas they express. Choice-based art education pedagogy is a broader, bolder approach to art education that emphasizes constructivist learning practices in specially designed learning environments tailored to meet the needs of individual learners. Teachers create dynamic learning situations when they harness their students' passions in choice-based art room settings. If content related to fantasy violence emerges from those activities, educators should not be afraid to integrate essential art education content during the course of those learning events. Talking to students about their thoughts and ideas related to fantasy violence allows teachers to understand the context of the content. Fantasy violence is a natural part of boys' emotional development and boys will flourish in schools where they are able to create art and express ideas related to their fantasy realms.

NOTE

1. Comment from Dr. John Crowe upon seeing a video of boys engaged in battle-drawing activity during *The Secret Art of Boys,* presentation at NAEA Conference, New Orleans, 2008: "Cy Twombly hasn't got anything on those boys."

REFERENCES

Brooks, J. G., & Brooks, M. G. (1999). *In search of understanding: The case for constructivist classrooms.* Alexandria, VA: Association for Supervision and Curriculum Development.

Brown, S. L., & Vaughan, C. C. (2009). *Play: How it shapes the brain, opens the imagination, and invigorates the soul.* New York: Avery.

Csikszentmihalyi, M. (1996). *Creativity: Flow and the psychology of discovery and invention.* New York: HarperCollins.

Cunningham, D. (1992). Beyond educational psychology: Steps toward an educational semiotic. *Educational Psychology Review, 4*(2), 165–194.

Douglas, K. M., & Hathaway, N. (2007, March). *Think about it: How school rebels and others find success in the choice-based art class.* Session presented at the 47th annual convention of the National Art Education Association, New York.

Douglas, K. M., & Jaquith, D. B. (2009). *Engaging learners through artmaking: Choice-based art education in the classroom.* New York: Teachers College Press.

Duncum, P. (1989). Unsolicited drawings of violence as a site of social contradiction. *Studies in Art Education, 30*(4), 249–256.

Fralick, C., & Gaw, C. (2008, March). *The secret art of boys.* Session presented at the 48th annual convention of the National Art Education Association, New Orleans, LA.

Gardner, H. (1983). *Frames of mind: The theory of multiple intelligences.* New York: Basic.

Gaw, C., & Douglas, K. M. (2010, March). *States of play in the choice-based art room.* Paper presented at the meeting of Child's Play, Children's Pleasures: Interdisciplinary Explorations, Hofstra University, Hempstead, NY.

Gurian, M., & Stevens, K. (2005). *The minds of boys: Saving our sons from falling behind in school and life.* San Francisco: Jossey-Bass.

Hathaway, N. (2008). 10 teaching and learning strategies in a "choice-based" art program. *Arts & Activities, 144*(1), 36–37.

Hollowell, P. (2008, June). Active shooter prevention matrix. *Law and Order: The Magazine for Police Management.* Available at http://www.hendonpub.com/resources/articlearchive/details.aspx?ID=206903

Jones, G. (2002). *Killing monsters: Why children need fantasy, super heroes, and make-believe violence.* New York: Basic.

Office of Juvenile Justice and Delinquency Prevention. (2008). *Juvenile arrest rate trends.* Available at http://www.ojjdp.ncjrs.gov/ojstatbb/crime/JAR_Display.asp?ID=qa05200

Kandel, E. R. (2006). *In search of memory: The emergence of a new science of mind.* New York: W. W. Norton.

Kindlon, D. J., & Thompson, M. (2000). *Raising Cain: Protecting the emotional life of boys.* New York: Ballantine.

Lowenfeld, V., & Britain, W. L. (1971). *Creative and mental growth.* New York: Macmillan.

May, R. (1975). *The courage to create.* New York: Norton.

Pinker, S. (2002). *The blank slate: The modern denial of human nature.* New York: Viking.

Rubin, J. A. (2005). *Child art therapy* (25th anniversary ed.). Hoboken, NJ: John Wiley.

Szekely, G. (2006). *How children make art: Lessons in creativity from home to school.* New York: Teachers College Press.

World Net Daily. (2007, August 22). *Youth suspended over sketch of gun.* Available at http://www.wnd.com/?pageId=43164

Part IV

THOUGHTS ON REFLECTION AND ASSESSMENT

Reflective teachers observe their students closely, question their practice routinely, and, like their students, ask "What if?" and "What next?" Learner-directed pedagogy transfers ownership of learning to the student. Educators, curious about the impact of shifting roles, look for evidence to demonstrate that students are developing critical and creative thinking skills while gaining knowledge through their work. Emergent behaviors, innovative use of materials and technologies, insightful connections, and collaborative ventures mark progress. The responsive practitioner processes these observations and explores instruction and assessment to empower and deepen learning.

Advocates of backwards design (Wiggins & McTighe, 2005) would insist on writing essential questions and developing assessments prior to designing curriculum activities. With emergent curriculum, however, assessments focus on core competencies inherent in creative work. To monitor student progress, Lois Hetland describes a method for observing and documenting students' growth in her chapter, "Can Studio Habits Help Teachers Assess Arts Learning?: Case of the King Cobra." The studio habits of mind (Hetland, Winner, Veenema, & Sheridan, 2007) provide a framework to assess creative and critical thinking skills. In a related system, Marvin Bartel describes reflective activities in "The Art of Motivation and Critique in Self-Directed Learning." Bartel advocates for thoughtful questioning to promote practice and inform mastery, leading to purposeful learning.

Teachers engaged in the next practice bring the learning process full circle, internalizing assessments to broaden their own understandings. In "The Important Thing," Dale Zalmstra beseeches teachers to focus on that which is essential by returning often to the very reasons they teach and the goals they embrace for their students. This part closes with Catherine Adelman's poem, "Approaches to Art," a window into one educator's thought process. Adelman seeks to define a place within the learning community as both facilitator and learner.

Contemplative educators counterbalance ambiguity with clarity of purpose. They observe, follow hunches, consider and weigh possibilities, and take initiative. Unforeseen outcomes and surprises reward their efforts to sustain learning through autonomy in the classroom.

REFERENCES

Hetland, L., Winner, E., Veenema, S., & Sheridan, K. (2007). *Studio thinking: The real benefits of visual arts education.* New York: Teachers College Press.
Wiggins, G., & McTighe, J. (2005). *Understanding by design.* New York: Prentice Hall.

CHAPTER 12

Can Studio Habits Help Teachers Assess Arts Learning?

Case of the King Cobra

Lois Hetland

Diane held her fingers to her lips. "Everyone's doing MCAS testing except us, and the kids are pretty wired." I had just arrived at Burr Elementary School to visit Diane Jaquith's choice-based visual art classroom. I'd met Diane on several occasions previously and heard wonderful rumors about her classroom, but you don't really know a teacher until you see her in action. I was eager to see what Teaching for Artistic Behavior meant in her hands.

The room was small, with a meeting-reading area bounded by shelving on two edges of a carpet. Surrounding that were table areas dedicated to different media: sculpture, drawing, collage, clay. Murals were a choice on this day; the wall by the sink was covered in roll paper, and kids stood in smocks with brushes, seriously at work. The room hummed, quieter today because of the classes taking standardized tests on either side. But if this was "wired," I'd be interested to see "in control"! All the students were focused on their work. That's one of the great advantages of choice-based art, of course—when kids can choose, they engage. When they're engaged, discipline problems melt away—who has time to act out when you're pursuing your own passions?

The class in progress was just wrapping up, and I settled at the clay table to watch the brief closure on the carpet and await the entry of the next group, a kindergarten class. They entered soon, and Diane quickly explained the mural option, and referred with a hand-wave to the other choices. Clearly, the students did not need explanation; they were entirely familiar with the classroom setup and ready to get to work. Sure enough, a small collection of 5-year-olds rushed to the clay table where I sat. The table was laid out simply, but the selected tools were elegant. Plastic yogurt cups held toothbrushes to facilitate "slip and score" for these small hands. One-foot boards had two layers of something cardboard-like that was duct-taped to each side so kids could easily roll slabs of even thickness. A garlic press was available for hairlike strings, along with a few wooden sticks and plastic knives. The table held simple, cheap tools chosen with care to meet the needs of young children.

And then he arrived, the boy I see so clearly in my memory. In my mind, I call him King Cobra Boy, or KC for short, because that was what he wanted most. "I want to make a King Cobra coming out of a basket!" he announced to no one in particular. He spoke rapidly, a machine-gun patter that continued without pause, accompanied by movement for all but three moments in the entire time he was at the center. "I can't make a King Cobra. I don't know how to make a King Cobra. I want to make a King Cobra. Can you help me make a King Cobra coming out of a basket? I don't know how to make a King Cobra coming out of a basket!" He looked at me imploringly as he reached for a ball of clay and began rolling it on the table. As it lengthened, he continued his worried monologue. "I don't know how to make a King Cobra. Can you help me make a King Cobra?" Two small balls of clay materialized from somewhere, and he stuck them on one end of the roll of clay, stuck his thumb in that end, and held it up to look. It was the first time I saw him still—he froze. Smiled. Set the coil down, and went right back to his ordered frenzy. "I need to make a basket for the King Cobra to come out of! I don't know how to make a basket for the King Cobra! Can you help me make a basket for the King Cobra to come out of?" This time, he took another ball of clay, rolled it round on the table, and looked around with both hands for something to help him make it into a basket. He spotted a tool, a stick with two round balls on either end, and this was the second pause. Freeze. Grab. He plunged the round end of the stick deeply into his ball of clay. His thumbs were too weak to push through on his own, but with the stick, he suddenly had—his basket. A third moment of stillness settled, and then the finale. He grabbed the clay snake in one hand, the basket in the other, and wrenched them together firmly. It was the moment of triumph. "I made a King Cobra coming out of a basket! I made a King Cobra coming out of a basket!" He spun in place, showing all who were around him, and they were amazed. A little clutch of peers gathered spontaneously to appreciate his work. "Wow. That's a great King Cobra!" The artist carefully wrote his name on the papers left for that purpose and set the paper and his cobra on the shelf.

I didn't see him again until the end of class, when Diane ran a quick sharing meeting on the rug. "Would anyone like to show what you did today?" she asked. KC desperately waved his hand in the air. I feared for the King Cobra's continued existence as it flopped precariously to and fro in his grip. "Please don't let that King Cobra break," I prayed. But the gods must have known King Cobra's importance, for it held together. "Does anyone have questions or comments?" Diane asked. "I like your cobra," a girl said. "Was it hard to make?" KC replied, "Well, no, er, yes, well, no, it was easy. But it was hard. It was pretty easy, but it was sort of hard." Class ended, the children left, and the room was just a room again without their vibrant presence.

It's easy to see the power in such a choice-based approach. Kids seek their own levels in a learner-directed classroom, each child finding his or her current growing edge. The challenge is to meet them at those edges and offer just enough help to keep them moving along. In KC's case, he may have enjoyed an assuring adult looking on, but despite his verbalized lack of confidence, he was truly independent. Perhaps he saw a glimpse of that more confident version of reality through this experience, or maybe he even truly learned it. But what if I hadn't been there at all? Or what if I'd "helped" him? I might have helped him well, or I might have done something that threw him off his own center. How can a teacher know in such situations what kids are learning and how to help them move along, through nudges or challenges or simple interventions like a new material?

I suggest that the *Studio Habits of Mind* (Hetland, Winner, Veenema, & Sheridan, 2007) are a perfect complement to a choice-based teacher's toolkit, because they allow teachers to see from a slight remove—but not too much. I've designed a Studio Thinking form (Figure 12.1) that guides ongoing assessment of student learning. The form frames teachers' observations and thinking about student learning using the categories of the Studio Habits of Mind. I am using it with art and general classroom teachers, both experienced and beginning, and it seems to be helping. Next, I model its use in relation to KC's case.

First, the teacher identifies a student of focus—who puzzles you? Who seems to need something more, or seems troubled or confused? Because teachers have so many students, and because those students are offering evidence of their learning with every decision they make in a constant stream of actions, a teacher can't use this form for every child every day or even every week. This analysis is more like strength training at the gym—it's to build the muscles for future work. So teachers need to be selective and strategic. Focusing on a child whose behavior and growth are puzzling gives insight into that child; but more, it helps to build teachers' capacities to see learning on the fly. Some teachers use the tool merely for developing that alertness. Others rotate students through, using the form to observe and analyze one or two students a day (or a week) in each class, in that way gathering data on all the students over time. In those moments when something memorable happens, the teacher can add that into the archive. When it's time to report

Figure 12.1. Ongoing Assessment: Analyzing Episodes of Student Learning with Studio Habits of Mind

Student: Date: Teacher:

What's an episode?: Anything students make, do, or say that reveals thinking. *Examples:* Portfolios of student work, observing students as they're working, interviewing students about their work or working behaviors.

Description of what teacher intended to be understood (learning goals):
Description and observations of the episode of learning:

Studio Habits: Consider and add to your observations in these categories.	*Understanding:* What do your observations suggest the student understands and doesn't?	What do you want to do next with and for the student?
Develop Craft		
Engage & Persist		
Envision		
Express		
Observe		
Reflect		
Stretch & Explore		
Understand Art World		

to parents, she has concrete data on which to base her evaluation. And, more importantly, she's kept track of what students need to grow in the moments of teaching and learning when her support can genuinely help.

After identifying a student, the teacher writes the date: May 3, 2007. And then she selects an "episode of learning." An episode can be pretty much anything. In this case, I observed a student during a class. But a teacher could review a portfolio of a student's work over time, or interview a child about his art, or look at a series of photos or drafts of the development of a single piece, or watch a video of the child at work. Whatever the episode, the teacher describes it first, as I did for KC. Often, though, it's not as long as my example—after all, I was writing for an audience who hadn't been there, while teachers write for themselves. The point is to describe what the episode was and what the teacher saw in it at first.

The next step is to run the episode mentally through each Studio Habit, asking, "What did I see in this episode that relates to (the habit under consideration)?" Following that, teachers ask themselves, "And what do those observations suggest that the student *does* and *does not* understand?" This move that translates observations categorized by Studio Habits into understanding—and *not* understanding—is critical for turning the observations toward decisions about teaching aimed to develop learning. Finally, after sieving all that data, the teacher comes to a decision about what to do next with and for that student. "Considering all this evidence, what do I most need to do now to help this student move forward?" Let's see how this plays out from the episode with KC.

DEVELOP CRAFT

KC has the skill to roll a lump of clay into a coil and to select and use a tool to punch a specific type of hole into a ball of clay. He did not slip and score, he did not pinch the ball to make the hole larger, and he did not texture the clay in any deliberate way with his fingers or tools (technique). He put his piece on the shelf with a paper for his name (studio practice).

Understanding: This suggests that KC has rudimentary skills with clay, but that he doesn't appreciate the importance of attaching clay to itself by slipping and scoring. It also suggests that, despite his apparent impulsivity, he is aware of the need to keep his work safe and identified, and he has the inclination and skill to do that.

ENGAGE AND PERSIST

KC is deeply engaged by the choice he has made—he came to class knowing what he wanted to make (alertness to finding ideas). He followed his passionate intention to its conclusion (inclination to persist), and he had enough skill to do that (despite his constant motion, which might confuse a casual observer into thinking he is disorganized, needy, or scattered).

Understanding: KC has a foundation for this disposition. I don't know what he would do if he were assigned a task, but I suspect that his attention might falter. His teachers can build on and expand his capacity to find his own interests and follow through on them.

ENVISION

KC had a clear idea of what he wanted to make, and he knew that clay was the material to fashion that vision. He seems to envision directly with the material, and not by drawing, for example. The fact that he paused when he saw the physical snake suggests to me that he was comparing it to the vision he had in his head and found it satisfying (this ties to observe and reflect: evaluate).

Understanding: KC may not understand that he envisions in his head and directly with the material, so if someone asks him to draw an idea, he might not be able to tell them that he works in this other way. Or, perhaps he does, given different conditions; it's worth watching for more evidence about that.

EXPRESS

KC's notion of expression seems quite tied to subject matter at this time. The *way* the snake was represented, beyond a rudimentary snakeness, didn't seem to matter too much. It needed eyes and a mouth, but no fangs or scales.

Understanding: KC seems not to understand (or perhaps it's that he doesn't care) the value of details for his creation and how he might use the medium of clay to express more about his ideas. He merely wants to express the essentials of the object he desired: a King Cobra in a basket. Surface textures were not essential, in his view; form is what matters in his expression.

OBSERVE

KC watched closely as his work developed in his hands. He saw when it had reached a "good enough" match to what he had imagined (envisioned). I wondered, but did not get any information, about whether he had seen a TV show or a photograph of a King Cobra in a basket. I suspect that his idea came from an observation of something.

Understanding: I wonder if KC understands that ideas come from observation? I could probe to find out. If he's ever stuck for an idea, I might try giving him some referents for things I know he's interested in, so that further observation might spark his ideas.

REFLECT

KC was able to convey ambiguity about the difficulty of the task in his response to a question. He also was able to articulate his worry about his capacity to do what he had seen in his mind, which turned out to be unnecessary. He also has a well-honed capacity to judge when he has satisfied his intention—he has a rudimentary disposition to evaluate his own work.

Understanding: I suspect that KC does not understand that his satisfaction is a judgment and that, as the artist, this is his to make. I would want to reinforce that from his experience so that he can come to value the inchoate feelings without words that help an artist to judge his own work.

STRETCH AND EXPLORE

KC has a particular strength in this area, perhaps by character or perhaps because of his developmental level. Whatever the reason, he was eager to play with the clay, move it around, see what happened, and take it from there. He seemed surprised by the success of the hole in the ball-that-became-a-basket; at first, he might have thought he'd made a mistake. But, if so, he saw its potential and immediately used it to his own ends.

Understanding: Again, I imagine KC does not realize how adept he is at this disposition to stretch and explore and use errors as sources of ideas. He did not demonstrate using errors diagnostically, and I'd want to probe that. In any event, I'd want to be sure to reinforce for him his strength in this Studio Habit, since otherwise he might not understand how important it is to his development as an artist.

UNDERSTAND ART WORLD

I saw no evidence that KC was making connections to any other works in the art world, though of course he might have been, as I might have found out with some questioning. But he certainly showed ideas about the community around him, both peers and adults. He sees the community as a source of help and of approval, as shown by his requests and responses to his peers.

Understanding: KC seems to see the community as a positive resource. I think he may not yet understand how he can use that resource as a source of new ideas.

NEXT STEPS WITH KC

What does KC need most right now to advance his learning in art? Based on this analysis, I think KC is making great strides on his own. Right now, his teacher could support him well by helping him recognize his strengths: his capacity to find what interests him; his habit of observing what's around him to spark ideas; his ability to follow that path to its logical conclusion; his capacity to play seriously with materials in order to find solutions that satisfy him; and the ways he makes connections with kids and adults as resources to him and he to them. Beyond that, I'd keep an eye out to see how to support these strengths with new resources and materials. He's running under his own steam, and my feeling is that as long as that's working, we ought to stoke the fire.

CONCLUSION

Information about learning surrounds teachers in classrooms every minute; everything students make, do, or say is a bit of evidence about the mystery of their learning. Through developing relationships with their students over the years, teachers become intuitively sensitive about responding in ways that urge students forward. We don't need to analyze every student every day to teach them well. But pausing to watch some students on some days, occasionally capturing a moment of learning in its richness and complexity, is useful in several ways. It can help teachers understand a student who is puzzling, and make reasoned choices about what to try next; it can help beginning teachers begin to see learning in their students' work and behaviors rather than seeing exploration as just "kids doing stuff"; and it can help us remember complexities we might have temporarily forgotten. Basically, observation reminds us that this studio we're in is full of students learning the nuanced attitudes and skills of thinking and acting as artists so that we can make better choices about how to support their development toward that vital goal.

REFERENCE

Hetland, L., Winner, E., Veenema, S., & Sheridan, K. M. (2007). *Studio thinking: The real benefits of visual arts education*. New York: Teachers College Press.

CHAPTER 13

The Art of Motivation and Critique in Self-Directed Learning

Marvin Bartel

What are your questions? In art, the more we learn, the more questions we have. A final exam in art is not a measure of what we know, but what we know that we want to learn. At the end of the course, if our students have learned to think and feel artistically, we can ask them what their questions are. If their thinking habits move forward productively, the class has been a success (Hetland, Winner, Veenema, & Sheridan, 2007). Those who do not have questions have not learned artistic thinking and feeling. The questions cannot be predicted, but these are the kind of questions I would hope for:

- What did I discover recently through my artwork? How did it happen?
- What do I want to work on in the future?
- What are the attributes I am seeking in my composition?
- What parts of my artwork are for myself? What parts are for others?
- What parts are motivated by empathy? What is for viewers?
- How much do I care about what others see in my work? Why?
- If the teacher did not show up, how would I change my artwork?
- What ways of working and thinking help me make discoveries?
- How are my observations informing my thinking and expression?
- What am I good at and most passionate about? What do I do well?
- What skills do I find most imperative to practice and improve?

Few children can be expected to ask these kinds of questions on their own. This behavior comes from having worked in a studio art culture where it is part of the creative process. Younger children say it differently, but often kindergarteners come up with the most profound and authentic truths about art:

- How can I know how to do it if I never did it before?
- What can be more art than me being myself?
- How can you know which one is better if you only try one thing?
- What are some of my favorite things that I could draw?
- Let's see, what did I forget to put in this picture?

How can a classroom culture produce end-of-term students who can be assessed on the basis of how evocative and original their questions have become? This is by no means a new issue in education. Josef Albers, artist and art teacher, said, "School should allow a lot to be learned, which is to say that it should teach little . . . Learning is better, because it is more intensive, than teaching: the more that is taught the less can be learned" (Borchardt-Hume, 2006, pp. 154, 155). Did Albers believe that education should be a bottom-up self-learning endeavor? Do we agree with Albers? If so, what is a teacher? Do we agree that art education should teach less so that more can be learned?

Questions and choices can cover a host of issues. Artists choose subject matter, theme, topic, art form, style, purpose, process, material, and every aspect of how and what we do. These questions direct and define our work. As art ideas materialize, more options, discoveries, refinements, and questions emerge. The studio art teacher is both top-down coach and learning colleague in a culture of self-directed bottom-up learning. We are in an apprentice/master relationship wherein the things being transmitted are much more than manual skills and techniques. We mentor a thought process that synthesizes relevant questions and imagines aesthetically evocative and expressive visual experiments.

MOTIVATIONAL INSTINCTS

While self-directed choice-making is natural in art education, every subject in every school benefits when students are engaged in their learning. Self-direction and choice-making give ownership. Student motivation increases when they take ownership in their own learning.

Often students are working on an assignment, but their demeanor, body language, behavior, and comments reflect boredom. This is common with required assignments that fulfill external standards. Sometimes we mistakenly assume that students will be more inspired and engaged if we show them a famous art example. Examples fail to produce motivation because they are more like answers than questions. The artists who originally created the exemplars, unlike our students, were probably engaged learners who chose their own problems. They were working to invent original work. Yet, when the thing is assigned as a project to make another one of those, motivation suffers. Motivation dies when assignments are framed more like answers to reproduce than like questions or problems that beg to be solved.

Artists work in response to questions and problems. Artists ask, "What if" questions. Studio art teachers manage laboratories in which to experiment and make discoveries. In student-directed learning, standards are learned as they are discovered through the work.

As artist-teachers, shouldn't we be able to read the minds and intentions of artists well enough to raise similar conundrums and puzzles within the minds of incipient artists in our classrooms? Could we reverse-engineer great exemplars from the art world in order to piece together the reengineering of the creative process within the minds of our students (Bartel, 2010)? Reverse engineering in art includes questions that bring out creative strategies and practice routines that assist in the mastery of media skills. However, like revealing the ending of a page-turner mystery, we can totally destroy the motivation to seek solutions if we reveal the answer in advance of solving the problem by first showing examples. As anti-intuitive as this may seem, there are better ways to motivate without showing exemplars and demonstrations. Artists are motivated when they wonder about things. Artists experiment. Artists are hands-on experiential learners. They practice skills. They learn from unexpected discoveries.

Daniel H. Pink (2009) writes about studies that explain motivation. According to Pink, workers are not so much motivated by their rate of pay (think grades in an art class), but by factors like worker *autonomy, purpose,* and their chance at *mastery.* The word *amp,* a common abbreviation for ampere, a unit of electric current, seems like an appropriate mnemonic for Pink's three intrinsic motivation factors. We need to remember that *autonomy, mastery,* and *purpose* can provide the electricity of motivation in studio art classes. Art students deserve a grade based on how much they learn, grow, and improve, but it is a mistake to see the grades themselves as basic motivation.

Games like Tetris, Sudoku, and the Rubik's Cube are popular because they appeal to our instinctive and intrinsic motivation for mastery. Many art skills such as observation drawing, realistic modeling, or forming clay on a potter's wheel provide intrinsic motivation if the student is aware of his or her own increasing skills and mastery based on good coaching and faithful practice. The innate desire for mastery motivates self-learning when the difficulty is reasonable and the goal is perceived to have value to the learner.

Autonomy

Autonomy asks each student to self-select the theme, method, subject, style, medium, and so on. In practice, student autonomy runs the risk of no new learning. It can be argued that autonomy, which is freedom to make one's own choices, allows students to avoid learning by electing to repeat their own past successes. This is autonomy without mastery and purpose. Teachers and parents may have trained children to follow directions, but very little else. In these situations, students have lacked coaching that fosters discovery-learning strategies, awareness-seeking pleasures, learning from mistakes, and so on. In spite of the many motivational benefits of autonomy, until students understand the methods and joys of new learning, total autonomy is overwhelming and frightening. Art teachers of self-directed art studio classes proactively cultivate a culture that builds ability and confidence with practice routines and reflection rituals that are difficult enough to be challenging, but easy enough to make progress without too much frustration. Autonomy motivates learning, innovation, and creativity when it is nurtured simultaneously with mastery, purpose, and recognition.

Mastery

Mastery can be elusive in a choice-based setting. Coaching mastery is somewhat like careful gardening in the sense that each situation may require special attention. The difficulty level of the questions and skills practice is adjusted to individual needs and abilities. In a choice-based setting there are not always rubrics and standards against which to compare—nor should there be. Self-directed learning implies that experiments and discoveries can open new questions and that pursuit of these questions produces mastery not previously defined. A greater degree of choice, autonomy, and creative thinking is perhaps best facilitated if we provide lists of open-ended questions rather than a list of previously determined standards. Can our questions begin at an easy entry level, but move toward greater challenge as we move down the list? Success may depend on whether the student is able to connect at an appropriate difficulty level. Later on we may wish to use a list of standards to double-check our question lists.

Mastery is dependent on focus and passionate practice. In traditional assignment-based art classrooms mastery is often assessed by comparison to some external model or by comparison to other students. In a choice-based classroom, practice and mastery are driven by discoveries and awareness dynamically brought to light. Mastery is anticipated, but not predefined. Often the artist-teacher, the peer group, and the individual collaborate in this discovery process. Practice routines are used both as time to gain art skills and as discovery time. Practice makes mastery easier. Practice also provides insights and ideas to use in planning and anticipation of a self-initiated project based on the practice.

Purpose

Purpose provides motivation as we learn and create what has importance beyond us. Art has many purposes. Yet, when I ask students about this, they can give me few reasons for art in the world. They have never consciously assessed the purposes of their artwork beyond the personal pleasure they get in producing it. Can we expect motivation when they are not aware of the reasons for learning? I do not recall seeing the Purposes of Art posted in studio art classes. Could such lists emerge organically during class critiques? For children and artists, personal purposes may differ from the grand purposes of art, but there are bound to be some connections and overlap. Every work can be discussed in terms of what it achieves for makers, as well as for viewers. Students who write statements that grow out of their artwork can identify the possible "whys" of their work. Discussions and critiques discover and identify the purposes in artwork. Could lists begin with the most obvious, but be extended to include every possible usage and function (both good and not so good)? For example, when art is used to persuade, it can be noble, or it can be extremely unethical.

As an artist, I am driven to learn and create when I feel that what I am doing will not get done unless I do it. I find purpose in being the one who has come up with the ideas. If I fail to express it, who will? To find motivation to write this paper, I need to feel that I am the person who needs to write it. I find little purpose in saying the same thing that has already been said by many other art teachers. Could this explain the boredom some students experience when "motivated" by exemplars?

Recognition

In addition to autonomy, mastery, and purpose, we strive for *recognition*. Recognition may be tied up in purpose and mastery, but as teachers we often see both benefits and pitfalls in giving a student special recognition for the purposes of motivation. Goldsmith (2005) illustrates this point for the business world: "When high impact performers are asked why they left an organization, many report, 'No one ever asked me to stay!' Many executives do not tell high-impact performers that they are special, for fear of alienating 'average' performers" (p. 4). Pay rate is not the most common response. In the classroom, student grades may not be as important as some assume.

Teachers have minute-by-minute opportunities to motivate with recognition. Recognition is not limited to formal grading, rubrics, awards, and exhibitions of student work. Affirmation is easy with top students. But unlike the workplace, school is for everybody. We are not trying to decide on whom to fire and whom to retain. Affirmation may be most effective for the average or low-performing students who seldom receive it. Students are all at different places in their artwork. We can find things to affirm at every level.

We should avoid simple praise. Top students often get unqualified praise to the point where some of them are confused and angered by it. To be helpful, recognition needs to be integrated into the discussions and exchange of ideas and questions about specific attributes in their work and work habits.

Virtually anything, when seen by a creative expert coach, may be returned to the student in the form of an affirmative open question. Upon observing mistakes, the temptation is to offer suggestions and corrections, though much of what we notice as mistakes can also be seen in a positive light. As a teacher, when I see a mistake, I may need to stop and reframe my response. I need to encourage the serendipity in the habitual, accidental, or incidental things that have happened in the work.

The primary goal is not the shortest route to a fine work of art, but the best route to a fine student, intensifying the passion to work, to search, to discover, and to learn. If I can find the right affirming and open questions that are meaningfully connected to a student's concerns, I have succeeded in bringing top-down coaching to bear on the student's bottom-up learning processes. On the other hand, if I merely point out mistakes and make suggestions, I am contributing to the student's learned helplessness by encouraging dependency. Dependency waits to be shown or told the "correct" way. Critique and motivation are systemically connected because the methods of mastery, the search for purpose, and defined affirmations are all part good critique methodology.

ART CRITIQUES TO ENHANCE SELF-LEARNING

Many art teachers are reticent about conducting critique. They fear negative feelings based on their own past bad experiences. They have found that fault-finding inquiry teaches students to make defensive arguments and justifications. It has not encouraged or motivated self-learning. They have not experienced good examples of positive discovery-based critique sessions.

In a choice-based environment, affirmative critique process is used to enhance motivation. The critique is designed to recognize and foster the positive aspects of experimentation, discovery, self-awareness, and knowledge construction. In a choice-based studio art culture the critique is not based on discipline-centered rubrics or external standards. The critique facilitates the ongoing search to sort out and help the producer identify individual constructs as they emerge. If and when an opportunity arises to connect with a traditional standard or art principle, this too becomes a discovery to celebrate and build upon.

Critiques that motivate self-learning through autonomy, mastery, purpose, and recognition are designed to encourage awareness and discoveries based on whatever happens in the work, whether intended or accidental. Regular group critiques by peers are cultivated as spontaneous as well as scheduled events. Scheduled critique rituals provide appropriate guidance and processes used to draw out discoveries. Teachers and peers use open questions to guide, coach, and build student curiosity and awareness of their own options and discoveries. Negative feedback is rigorously avoided and mistakes are seen as serendipities and opportunities.

EMPATHIC OPEN QUESTIONS

When considering critique, we realize that coaching for self-learning refrains from making suggestions (suggestions encourage dependence on experts), refrains from being negative (negative critique shuts down inspiration), refrains from empty praise (it is frustrating, confusing, and useless), and refrains from prejudging (it is disrespectful and often erroneous). Instead, we put the emphasis on empathetic open questions that search for cause and effect, for new awareness, and for the facilitation of self-enlightenment.

Empathy is among the noblest of human instincts. Empathy is the heart of art and art instruction. During the creation of art we are constantly using empathy to imagine how others will perceive our work. If a teacher learns the student's concerns and intentions, it helps teaching become empathic. We are better able to connect to what practice may be relevant and what purposes are being achieved. The student becomes empowered. "Teaching depends on what other people think . . . not what you think" (Loewenberg Ball, 2010, p. 7). In critique, we must do the same in considering how the student perceives the critique process. Teachers and peers make no assumptions, but they notice many things. They make many inquiries to clarify, become better informed, and build awareness.

Open questions provide an empathic way to be helpful. Discovery and awareness-building critiques use open questions that stress the desire to learn on the part of the questioner. Affirmative and neutral observation questions might ask for what you see, what you notice first, what meanings you imagine, what feelings you experience, how something was done, how was an idea originated, and so on. Follow-up questions are analytical questions to inform our understanding of cause and effect. We ask for clarification of how an effect was produced, whether it was intentional or not. The use of nonjudgmental questions is intended to help everybody build awareness, make discoveries, and increase our mastery of art. The purpose of a discovery-based critique is not to call the maker of the work or the artwork into question. The purpose is to illuminate through discovery—to enlighten and learn together. It is affirmative because learning has been successful, and mastery and purpose have been recognized, identified, and affirmed.

If the maker overlooked or did not find something important, the viewer phrases a helpful question. For example, I do not say that the top right section of a painting seems dead and unfinished. Instead, I ask which parts of the painting appear to be the most finished and effective? In civil society, and in the studio art classroom, it is counterproductive to be directly negative or nasty. When being an empathic teacher or peer, one can be honestly positive or neutral and achieve awareness goals while avoiding defensiveness, sadness, hostility, and discouragement.

Critique, when properly coached and cultivated, becomes a significant part of the studio classroom culture that motivates and inspires. When critique succeeds, it honors student *autonomy*, it informs *mastery* by coaching the practice of becoming more aware and discerning, and it helps students discover *purpose* in their efforts and achievements. When we avoid critique, we are depriving students of much of the self-learning that could happen in a studio art class.

The wise teacher thinks of critique as a way of converting experiments, mistakes, accidents, and sincere practice into a time of awareness, discovery, focus, direction, persistence, reflection, concept construction, and mastery. It is a time to find and phrase questions, and form new theories and hypotheses to test. Critique is a process of mutual inquiry leading to the discovery of individual and group identity and purpose. Studio art critique sessions are not debate episodes with winners and losers. Studio art classroom critique processes should be anticipated as a walk in the woods, a visit to a botanical garden, or a visit to a zoo full of new delights, discoveries, and learning. Critique is anticipated as a motivational and inspiration-finding activity.

THE ONE-ON-ONE CRITIQUE

Opportunities for one-on-one critique are common in a high school, but even with younger children many opportunities arise. Students frequently seek counsel deciding if something is finished, what are the next steps, or in selecting something for the school exhibit. When faced with these brief mini-critiques, it is easy to make a quick suggestion instead of helping a student learn how to gain mastery.

Questioning is a teaching skill that most of us have to develop. Here is a list of principles I have found useful (Bartel, 2004):

- Phrase *observation, clarification,* and *descriptive* questions that ask students to make positive choices from within artwork. For example, we can ask which areas are noticed first, or which seem more three-dimensional. As an artist/teacher, I have been looking at my own work from both negative and positive perspectives. I often see the negatives first. However, in conducting critique, I rephrase my thoughts to affirm the positive and allow the student to discover the weaknesses.
- Observation and clarification are followed by analytical questions about how and why we think things worked. Follow-up questions encourage elaboration and additional discoveries. For example, ask why they think so, and where else this happens. Ask what makes it work, and how they thought of it. General principles are often discovered when the reasons for noticing something are discovered.
- Meaning, interpretation, and feeling questions often give purpose to the work. We can ask for speculation and for guesses. We can ask for possible titles. We can even ask for opposites as a creative way to get at the meaning, expressive qualities, and feelings of an artwork.
- Avoid questions that intend to zero in on problems. For example, it may sound accusatory to ask why these two things are next to each other. It is more affirmative to ask which juxtapositions work best together.
- Use open questions so that multiple feasible answers are acceptable. This allows for and encourages creative looking, thinking, and choices. These are often what, how, and why questions. Responses to open questions frequently reveal things that teachers would have missed.
- Avoid the yes/no question game that tries to get the student to guess the teacher's hidden agenda.

- When working with student-directed learning, questions and comparisons come out of the work that the student brings to the critique. Many questions cannot be known before we see the materialized work.

I find it helpful when students show me more than one example of their artwork. This allows me to ask the student to look at a certain attribute in two or more similar works. For example, when conducting a one-on-one critique of two or three pieces of similar pottery, I can ask the student about a particular aspect while using affirmative terminology. I can ask which one works better and follow with a question that elicits an explanation. On a piece of pottery we might compare the foot rim treatment, the top edge treatment, the handle size, the handle thickness, the handle shape, the handle placement, the height and width proportions, the surface qualities, the tonal relationships, the feeling emitted, the practical features, the uniqueness, or the personality of the work. I often begin by asking the student to tell me which of the pieces seems most innovative and creative, and then ask for an analysis of the reasons. Can the student explain it? Sometimes it may be appropriate to ask which one has a stronger sense of unity. This is followed by a "how" or "why" question to help clarify. Similar comparative queries can deal with variety, with images, with meaning, with style, and with feeling.

Some students are habitually self-deprecating. They dwell on mistakes in a self-defeating way. I mention that I often make many mistakes, especially when I am learning something new. I even make mistakes when I should know better. I explain that it feels bad. So sometimes I practice more, or I have to turn off the radio as I work, but I always hope that the mistake or accident turns out to be a great discovery. Mistakes help me think of a new idea or approach that I could never have imagined on my own. Can we allow our mistakes and accidents to talk to us? Do they ask and answer the questions that we forgot to ask? I might ask, what happened here that you could not have seen before. What else does it suggest? What are some other ways to use it? A mistake may reveal a new purpose for the work, as at the time when a soft clay vase fell on the floor. I looked at it and noticed a way to make vases to hang on the wall.

Seeing two or more similar works from the same student helps me empathize when searching for what the student is learning, discovering, and/or could be learning and discovering. The standard rubric question of how well the work follows the assignment is seldom useful. However, affirmative discovery learning questions are always there when I see two or more related examples from a student.

This is not the "sandwich" method where the teacher starts with something positive, then gives the "meat" of the critique (the negative comment), and then tops it off with another compliment (students really only remember the bad stuff in such a system). This is a positive, positive, positive discovery method. If it is a sandwich, it has two pieces of chocolate cake with frosting in the middle. One work is often stronger in only some respects, while the other work is stronger in other respects. Since the same student did both works, every student can receive positive recognition and affirmation in every part of this teaching/learning exchange. It is considerably more difficult to use a consistently positive approach when reviewing a single work by the student.

When two or more works are compared, students learn to use *positive comparative awareness*. They naturally imitate the process on their own as they work. Their discoveries evolve faster. They are learning an important artistic self-directed behavior. Art itself is an evolving subject. Learning art is like searching for a moving target. Learning art is based on experiments, questions, and discoveries within a context of person, time, and place.

Similar discussions can be encouraged on a peer-to-peer basis. Student teams can collaborate to compete with other teams to develop lists of relevant attributes and questions for each art form typically produced in a particular studio art class. For every visual and aesthetic attribute there is a list of affirmative questions with which to gain awareness. By setting up a system of competing teams and assigning points to unique question topics, students will instinctively work harder to produce a greater variety and diversity of questions.

The same critique strategies can also be practiced when discussing well-established art exemplars that relate to what students have created. When discussing and comparing works by an established artist whose work is in some way related to what the students have been working on, students will feel empowered to speculate on what an artist was thinking and feeling. They can guess what questions and issues an artist may have been working on. Contrary to popular practice, discussions of art history and contemporary art exemplars might be more fruitful when conducted after students have worked on their own similar questions and experiments. Students who have struggled with similar problems will be more likely to empathize with the concerns of the artist.

CONCLUSION

Self-directed learning is a lifelong habit. It is nurtured in an empathic culture of imagination, practice, inquiry, experimentation, discovery, and critique. Self-assigned practice, projects, and reflections replace teacher assignments and preliminary examples. In bottom-up learning with top-down coaching, directed hands-on practice sessions and small sample-making sessions replace most teacher demonstrations to introduce new processes. Affirmative inquiry-based critique uncovers discoveries and drives continued inquiry, thus building awareness and sequenced learning. Students have more questions at the end because they know more and because they appreciate the ways in which good questions inspire new learning and evocative work.

REFERENCES

Borchardt-Hume, A., Ed. (2006). Albers and Moholy-Nagy: Artists' writings, in *Bauhaus to the new world*. pp. 154–162. London: Tate Modern.

Bartel, M. (2010). *Reverse engineering creative strategies*. Available at http://www.bartelart.com/arted/reverse.html

Bartel, M. (2004). *Encouraging creative thinking with awareness and discovery questions*. Available at http://www.bartelart.com/arted/questions.html

Goldsmith, M. (2005). *Retain your top performers*. Available at www.smithcp.com/PDFS/RetainEmployersArticle.pdf

Hetland, L., Winner, E., Veenema, S., & Sheridan, K. M. (2007). *Studio thinking: The real benefits of visual arts education*. New York: Teachers College Press.

Loewenberg Ball, D. (2010, March 2). Quoted in E. Green, Building a better teacher. *New York Times*. Available at http://www.nytimes.com/2010/03/07/magazine/07Teachers-t.html?pagewanted=1&em

Pink, D. H. (2009). *Drive: The surprising truth about what motivates us*. New York: Penguin Group.

CHAPTER 14

The Important Thing

Dale Zalmstra

What if this week in art is the only week I will have with this child? What if this child moves to another school that doesn't have art? *This could be it.* I think about things like this.

My school is like a lot of urban elementary schools—lively and wonderful, with rich diversity. The children come from homes where about 45 different languages are spoken. They and their parents have backgrounds that I can only partially imagine. Yes, there is poverty and our mobility rate is high. I see my students for a week at a time in our year-round schedule, and often many weeks pass before their art class comes back in rotation. On Sunday nights I print out rosters of my classes for the week because, inevitably, there will be new students added and others who will have moved on.

What if this week in art is the only week I will have with this child? I see my students less and less as our school grows. *This really could be it.* The question I keep asking myself is, what do I want the students to take away from their time here? What is the Important Thing?

There is a picture book by Margaret Wise Brown (1990) called *The Important Book*, which gives focus to this train of thought. It is written with a simple pattern that states the important thing about something, describes several more attributes, and then reiterates the important thing. What is grass? What is an apple? What is a spoon? Using the pattern in *The Important Book*, I look at my teaching practice to identify what is most important for my students to learn.

THE IMPORTANT THING

The Important Thing for my art students is that they love art and consider themselves artists.
Students need time for discovery.
Students need to have ownership.

Students need opportunity to reflect.
But the Important Thing for my students is that they love art and
    consider themselves artists.

As teachers, we are inundated with information, curriculum, and philoso-
phies. For our own sakes, and for the quality of our teaching, it is vital that
we continue to examine what is most important in our teaching. Why do we
do what we do? This simple pattern, from Wise Brown's book, provides a
vehicle to look at our teaching practices, and provides a structure to reflect
and share about our practice.

   ***The Important Thing for my art students is that they love art and
consider themselves artists.*** The challenge for me is to figure out what it
means to be an artist and love art and how to make it happen in my classroom. I started with: What is an artist? How does an artist work? As I got
to know my school and I became more experienced at teaching, I knew I
wasn't reaching all of the kids all of the time. Based on my own questions
and observations in trying to figure out best teaching practices, I decided to
transform my classroom into a choice-based art studio. This was my first
step in creating a path for all of my students to find their individual ways to
love art and be artists.
   My classroom studio resembles other learner-directed environments.
The goal for the talk/demo/lesson at the beginning of class is to be brief—5
minutes. At the beginning of the week we do work as a whole class on skill-
builders or ways to develop ideas, or take time to look at the work of others.
The majority of time is saved for open studio when students can work in
areas previously introduced or try new ideas and materials.
   Students work with media and ideas of their choosing, and learn in the
way that works best for them. The choice-based classroom offers full differentiation. Students with unique situations immediately become a working
part of the group, because everyone is working in their own way. Asking
new students about their favorite art media or who they would like to work
with, and letting them start from there, provides a level of comfort in a new
environment. If students don't speak English at all, or very little, it is easy
to visually communicate. They can work with the same level of autonomy
as the rest of the class. New students can follow and work with peers, often
choosing to work with subjects and materials with which they are already
familiar. In this same way, students with learning differences can work at
their level with materials that work best for them. The teacher comes to
know that certain students will be drawing, or painting, or part of the huge
contingent of kids who thrive on being able to work three-dimensionally.
I have come to treasure and nurture those who love drawing because this

is often a short-lived phase. My goal is for students to go as far as they want with a particular media while they are still passionate about it. Students pursue their interests in the working style that works best for them. Some students prefer to work independently, some like to work in groups, while others like both ways of working. This is an environment conducive to spontaneous collaborations. Young leaders and art directors emerge in the process of working together to negotiate both process and product. A lovely benefit is that in the choice-based classroom, management becomes much easier. I am able to observe students and take my cues from them. I can see what they need to learn in order to accomplish their ideas, and what artist or culture they would benefit from knowing more about. I look for what could be their next step.

How do I know that the basic structure of my art program, and how it has evolved, is meeting curricular goals? My analysis, through observation and reflection, is that there are three areas in particular that are essential in facilitating the Important Thing for my students. The first is time for *discovery*. The second is for students to have *ownership* of their work. The third is opportunity to *reflect*.

Students need time for discovery. Discovery is a time for play and exploration in the studio. Discovery happens when time is given for developing skills of perception and learning to make connections between what you see and do, think and know. It is time for incubation, letting an idea have time to develop. As teachers, one of the most important things we can do is to protect our students' time for discovery. Children learn through play and exploration. Students actively acquire and store bits and pieces of learning, and save them, and figure out how to use them. This learning becomes part of the student. Artists also know this and how to develop ideas through time and play. I need to be fierce in protecting this time for my students. Because. Because it is the antithesis of what our schools are about, because it is difficult to quantify. It is the pause, the time in between, the waiting time that is so important; it can be quiet or loud or active or contemplative. Learning rarely evolves from point A to point B in a straight line; it is usually a line that meanders all over the place. Time for discovery is not the whole artistic process, but it is an essential organic part that should never be undercut or disregarded.

Students need to have ownership. Ownership is a key aspect of my Important Thing, essential to loving art and being an artist. Students' ownership of themselves as artists and ownership of their art and time are developed in this forum. If they cannot think for themselves and be responsible for developing their own ideas and related skills, then students are not the artists—the teacher remains the artist. Ownership is developed with the ability to choose, follow passions, and express ideas and feelings in works that have personal relevance. In addition, having the choice to work independently or in collaboration, and having opportunities to develop the discipline of learning and craftsmanship, lead to ownership. To be an artist, one acts like an artist and works like an artist.

Students need opportunity to reflect. My mind thinks in terms of complex webs of information and relationships, and so I often used to think that my students were also aware of this interconnectedness. I now understand that, more often than not, they are rarely making similar connections. It has taken me a long time to internalize this and shift my teaching accordingly. I need to wrest time away from their artmaking to make sure that they have time to reflect. They need time to talk, to think, and to share so they can grasp the big picture and see how they and their art connect to the world.

But the Important Thing for my art students is that they love art and consider themselves artists. As the teacher, one of the best ways of evaluating what I am doing is to ask myself the question, "Who is the artist?" If the answer is often me, the teacher, then I need to rethink what I am doing. Asking questions informs my teaching in my own self-talk; but it is also key in interactions with my students. When I am asked a question by a student (about a million times a day), I try to respond with a question. For me, this continues to be a challenge, but it puts responsibility for learning back on the student artist and provides opportunity for discovery. If the art comes from the students, they own it and they have an opportunity to love it. The challenge is to keep what is most important for my students and myself front and center in my classroom and in my curriculum. My own self-checks are to continuously evaluate and ask:

- Who is the artist?
- Have I allowed time for discovery in my planning?
- How am I giving the students ownership?
- Am I asking questions more and giving answers less?
- Have I created time to reflect in useful ways?
- When I assess, am I assessing what is actually important to my goals?
- Do I communicate these concepts clearly to students?
- Do I communicate these concepts clearly to my school community so that what is important stands strong?

CONCLUSION

It is not necessary that we, as teachers, have the same Important Thing—each of us has our own Important Things. Margaret Wise Brown's pattern is simple to say, but a challenge to do. It is valuable to figure out for ourselves what matters most and determine the best way to get there. The Important Thing can be a tool to evaluate decisions that impact your art program. Design your curriculum and structure teaching and learning with your Important Thing front and center. Continually evaluate your practice. Staying attuned to the Important Thing can ground and empower us as teachers. If this week in art is the only week I will have with these children, then what they take away is theirs to keep. These children are aware that they have independently made discoveries and learned as a result, and can continue doing so wherever they go.

REFERENCE

Wise Brown, M. (1990). *The important book*. New York: HarperCollins.

Approaches to Art

Catherine Adelman

Approaches to art
Get to the point!
Summon that intermediary inventive mind
What is the essence of this artistic experience?
Why this now?
How will this allow you to make sense
develop new abilities
construct knowledge
find meaning for yourself?

What are the ideas, images and words within the discipline
from the rich store of human experience
in the power of natural forms
that will make a connection with you
and give us a place to begin?

Making art
interacting with materials
forming and reforming
adapting tools to a specific task
the immediacy of sensory experience
movement and touch
memory and thought
imagination and feeling
All are equal players in this concentrated work

In the continuous push and pull
countless choices are made
The work flows from this synergy within
The engagement of mind, body and spirit

with matter
solid and fluid
This artmaking is a wholesome process

When do I push you to go further
to make harder choices?
Where is the conviction in your insistence
that you are finished?

Who are you?
You are at the center of this work
both mine and yours
I know you each by name
We meet and gather on the floor all forty-five of you
Some of you are sitting in rows
I face you from the front of the room
Some of you are seated in clusters
facing every which way
Sometimes we meet in small groups
And work in whatever space we can find

We defy the oppressive organization of space and time called school
And do this art together!

You are there with your point of view
Your stories, your questions
Most of the time you are ready
for the adventure
Sometimes you are there with your pain
At every turn I learn
what it means to be inclusive
and still hold you to the task at hand
This challenges me

This teaching is an act of faith
I believe in your ability to do original work
in your generative and creative capacity of mind

You will need these powers later
to make meaningful choices in life
to discover possibilities in the everyday
to find your voice and the courage to speak your mind

to know when to listen and how to learn for a lifetime
to fully participate in the life of the community
to join in the fray

I celebrate your effort, your unique potential
Is that coming across in how I stand here and speak
and share this time with you?
Where is William's happy tact for the concrete moment
and that ingenuity in meeting and pursuing the pupil?

I hold this potential space open for you
To express how you feel about what you know
To make discoveries and find some personal truth
This is the site of cultural experience.

When the making is complete
we stand back to see
what meaning you have made with marks
It's a wonder!

   The poem, "Approaches to Art," came to me whole in the summer of
1993 after months of pondering. It was my contribution to the curriculum project for The Roots of Modernism in Twentieth Century American
Arts and Culture, an institute for educators sponsored by the Maine Collaborative at Bowdoin College the previous summer. My participation in
the institute gave me the opportunity to think deeply about my professional
practice and make connections to contemporary thought regarding teaching
and learning.
   Through the intervening years, the poem has stood as a statement of
personal belief. I have found new meaning in the poem, as my ideals and
beliefs regarding teaching and learning in art education take form and find
expression in Teaching for Artistic Behavior. Most important, I believe my
students realize lasting benefits in their art education as they discover their
strengths, pursue their chosen interests, and develop their own artistic practices.

About the Editors
and the Contributors

THE EDITORS

Nan E. Hathaway holds a B.A. in Art and a M.A. in Special Education–Gifted and Talented. She is a licensed art educator, K-12, currently teaching at the middle school level in Duxbury, Vermont. She frequently speaks at state and national art education conferences about creativity, giftedness, and learner-directed art education. She is the author of several articles, past Chair of the National Association for Gifted Children Creativity Network, and contributor to a monograph about creativity, *Perspectives in Gifted Education: Creativity.*

Diane B. Jaquith is a longtime K–5 art teacher in Newton, Massachusetts, and a co-founder of Teaching for Artistic Behavior, Inc., a choice-based art education advocacy organization. She is a co-author, with Katherine Douglas, of *Engaging Learners Through Artmaking: Choice-Based Art Education in the Classroom*, and several articles about choice-based pedagogy and creativity. She is a frequent speaker at regional and national conferences and serves on the Cross-Division Research Committee of the National Art Education Association.

THE CONTRIBUTORS

Catherine Adelman is an artist and an educator who recognizes the source of her own creativity in the imaginative play of early childhood, when she spent summers on a barrier island and the rest of the year in an urban landscape. She has worked as a teacher and director of an alternative school, and is currently a public school art teacher in rural Maine, where she has taught for 18 years.

Marvin Bartel, Ed.D., Emeritus Professor of Art, Goshen College, is an artist, inventor, and has been an art teacher for over 40 years. As an art educator, he has written more than 100 articles for art teachers and parents, many of which are posted at his Art and Learning to Think and Feel website. He has made conference presentations in art education, consulted for schools, and led art teacher in-service sessions in Colorado, Nebraska, Missouri, Indiana, Michigan, Wisconsin, New Jersey, and Brazil. He has invented, patented, and built unique fuel-efficient pottery kilns, and he produces work exhibited in regional, national, and international venues.

Katherine M. Douglas has a B.S. in Education from the University of Maryland and a M.A. in Integrated Studies from Cambridge College. A co-founder of Teaching for Artistic Behavior, Inc., which supports teachers practicing choice-based art education, Douglas has collaborated in international online educational mentoring projects using technology to connect teachers and students. She is a co-author, with Diane Jaquith, of *Engaging Learners through Artmaking: Choice-Based Art Education in the Classroom.* She was named Massachusetts Distinguished Art Teacher in 2005.

Ellyn Gaspardi teaches at the middle school level in Bridgewater, Massachusetts, and is an adjunct professor at Cambridge College in the Education Department. Previously she worked for 5 years in social services with children who had been severely abused emotionally and physically. Ellyn holds a B.F.A. from Syracuse University and a M.Ed. from Lesley University in Integrated Arts and Curriculum Development.

Clyde Gaw spent most of his early childhood playing rough-and-tumble games with his four brothers and sister, drawing battle pictures, building forts, and fashioning crude hunting weapons out of objects he found in surrounding industrial sites near his boyhood home of Walkerton, Indiana. He is currently the art teacher at New Palestine Elementary School in central Indiana, a position he has held for over 25 years. He serves on the Advocacy Advisory Committee for the National Art Education Association, and is the advocacy advisor for the Art Education Association of Indiana.

Lois Hetland, Ed.D., is a co-author of *Studio Thinking: The Real Benefits of Visual Arts Education* and an Associate Professor of Art Education at the Massachusetts College of Art and Design. As research associate for Project Zero at Harvard Graduate School of Education, she is currently Principal Investigator for a pilot learning for understanding project in Alameda County, California. She previously served as Co-principal Investigator for a Wallace Foundation-funded project, the Qualities of Quality: Excellence in Arts Education and How to Achieve It. She has authored numerous articles and professional development series on the arts and understanding. Prior to her work in arts education and research, she was a classroom teacher for 17 years.

Pauline Joseph holds both a B.A. and M.A. in Fine Arts from the University of Wisconsin, Madison and studied art education at the University of Wisconsin, Milwaukee. Joseph taught art in public schools for 39 years and has been a visiting lecturer at the University of Massachusetts, Boston and Massachusetts College of Art and Design. Joseph, a co-founder of Teaching for Artistic Behavior, Inc. was named Massachusetts Art Teacher of The Year in 2002.

Tannis Longmore holds a B.F.A. in Illustration from Parsons School of Design in New York and completed graduate studies in Early Childhood and Elementary Education at Bank Street College. For 20 years, she has taught as both a classroom teacher and art specialist in early childhood and elementary settings. Currently an art teacher in the Stafford Public Schools, Connecticut, she has written and illustrated two children's picture books: *Little Pig and the Blue-green Sea* and *Adrianna and the Magic Clockwork Train*.

Linda Papanicolaou is a graduate of Skidmore College, studied art education at Teachers College, Columbia University, and holds a Ph.D. in art history from New York University. She taught art history at New York area colleges and worked for the Metropolitan Museum of Art. She has taught after-school art and ceramics classes and elementary art for the Palo Alto school district, and currently teaches at Terman Middle School. She has been a choice-based teacher for 5 years, is a published poet, and the editor of a haiku journal, *Haigaonline*.

Cameron Sesto has been the art specialist for Stoneridge Children's Montessori School in Beverly, Massachusetts for 12 years. Trained as a photographer at Rochester Institute of Technology, she is also a self-taught oil painter, printmaker, sculptor, and writer. She is the author of *Sticks, One End Open*, and *Simply Great*.

George Szekely has been a pioneer in developing creative changes and methodologies for art teaching for 35 years. He was among the first art educators to emphasize the importance of children's play in artmaking and to advocate the study of children's home art as the foundation for school art practice. A prolific author and artist, he has been Area Head and Senior Professor of Art Education at the University of Kentucky since 1978.

Ilona Szekely earned her Ph.D. in the Department of Educational Policy Studies and Evaluation at the University of Kentucky, and is Assistant Professor of Art Education at Eastern Kentucky University. Her doctoral research focuses on art education in museum settings. She has worked at the Metropolitan Museum of Art in New York, at the New Museum, and in children's galleries in New York and Washington, DC. She has published papers and exhibited her artworks both nationally and in England and Australia.

Dale Zalmstra holds a M.Ed. from Lesley University, Cambridge, Massachusetts and National Board Teacher certification. She has taught for 9 years at the elementary level, 7 of those in a choice-based classroom. She is a frequent speaker at state and national art education conferences, and has assisted with the organization of professional conferences for the Colorado Art Education Association and ArtSource Colorado.

Index